Lost Treasures
of the
Tropical Variety

by

Arthur Kingtide

www.tropicalvariety.com

Arthur Kingtide

Summary

Lost Treasures of the Tropical Variety explores a mysterious realm encompassing billions of dollars in lost artifacts, loot, and priceless heritage sunken leagues below the seas hundreds of years ago. Central focus aims toward tropical and subtropical areas around the world with remarkable discoveries, though several articles are interspersed with historical legends which took place outside of tropical zones.

A vast body of known wealth remains to be found, and likely there is much more unknown yet to be discovered. Here is a warm thanks to those brave souls risking their lives to uncover secrets of our nautical past.

Underwater explorers redefine the way we look at history by finding lost knowledge in artifacts, relics, and treasures trapped by the seas of time.

Lost treasures are not only highly valued for their weight in precious metals or gems, but also for historical significance. Cultures around the world reclaim irreplaceable heritage with every rediscovery, and the information provided by the treasures is unparalleled insight into the past.

Treasures of the Tropical Variety is a guidebook designed to recount historical facts of lost ocean riches observed from new perspectives, and stimulate further contribution to restoring world marine heritage by sharing this research. By protecting lost treasures of our past, we can better understand who we are, and learn how exploration and determination of our ancestors brought us to where we are today.

All values of treasure mentioned throughout this book are approximated in United States dollars unless otherwise stated. Fair market conversions at the time of writing this book were used in all calculations and may not explicitly include the respective country's intrinsic value for reclaiming its lost heritage.

Irreplaceable lives, heritage,
and treasure lost at sea.

Table of Contents

Introduction

Pristine, relaxing tropical getaways band across the Equator between Tropic of Capricorn and Cancer like a beam of sunlight fusing two halves of Earth together. Favorable weather, warm temperatures, beautiful scenery, and white sand beaches are just a few reasons people really enjoy spending vacation time in these areas.

Lush landscapes, heavenly horizons, and surreal sunsets aren't the only treasures Earth's tropics have to offer though. Much more is hidden from plain view, nestled beneath an ocean crest among seas of coral and exotic marine life, lost to time for hundreds and even thousands of years. For as long as people have visited and lived in tropical areas the ocean finds ways to reclaim precious treasures once safely tucked in the pockets of man.

Trading operations have long depended on fair tides for transporting goods. Sailing vessels made port in places previously unfathomable to reach by land, playing crucial roles in expanding empires gaining new territory while helping to move resources around the planet.

Livelihood of entire nations and their citizens depended on prosperity of shipping fleets hundreds of years ago just as in the modern world, with a lucrative promise to readily obtain more resources and sustain large populations. Ocean trading routes connecting distant civilizations brought many benefits by expanding horizons, increasing knowledge, and advancing technologies. For this increased convenience however, there is a price.

The sea is a beast in its own right, with promises of new found wealth from distant lands, secretly stowing misery, misfortune, and servitude to false hope. Facing the oceans meant not only overcoming severe weather such as typhoons, hurricanes, and endless miles of unpredictable waters, but it also entails dealing with a threat of unexpected guests prepared at arms to take the ship, its goods, and dispatch the crew as quick as the blink of a pirate's eye.

Weather and atmospheric conditions continuously play important roles crossing open waters by ship. Frightening patterns develop, such as rogue waves, williwaws, and microbursts threatening both severe damage or vessel capsizing in a moment's notice. When conditions are just right, a pleasant sail becomes a life-threatening event, not to mention water looks the same in every direction! Long days aboard a rocking ship passing in and out of stormy seas are sure to get the best of any mariner.

As history points out repeatedly, a number of vessels succumbed to the deep blue's calling, meeting an end in free fall to the ocean floor. Then, at the bottom of the sea, they face the ocean's ultimate grasp, trapped over time in sediment and bits of coral, creating new homes to future generations of marine life.

Unfavorable weather plays a predominant role in the tales of many ships lost at sea, working synonymously with the deep blue calling. The added dynamic further complicates navigation by masking reefs, rocky outcrops, and sand banks in swishing swirling ocean swells, and subjecting ships to stormy situations too dangerous for even the most weathered of captains. Perhaps legends of the Kraken are in part metaphorical descriptions of threatening weather on the ocean, to grasp the largest of ships and snap it in two, eating the ship and crew.

Shipwrecks serve but another purpose should a bold adventurous band of modern explorers toil long hours with their lives at risk to find, dive upon, and recover artifacts lost to ancient ocean perils. At times those dangerous situations lead to new discoveries which may prove old legends and their treasures to finally be true. Considering the sheer number of myths and legends, only a fraction of lost artifacts have been successfully recovered, and many still lurk deep in dark shimmering waters for later discovery.

Each cache reclaimed from below unforgiving seas further demonstrates a possibility to recover the treasure of a lifetime, gracefully fueling motivations of new-age treasure hunters without hesitation. To whom we ask, could this fever be attributed to?

Nearly two-hundred years ago, an archaeological pioneer named Heinrich Schliemann stubbornly and relentlessly argued with scientists, profoundly claiming existence of ancient Greek settlements mentioned in Homeric epics to be poetic truths. Heinrich's stubbornness lead to the research and excavations of several important sites now recognized by UNESCO World Heritage. Sites such as ancient Greece's legendary city of Troy, for example.

Schliemann started an archaeological revolution, and his discovery of Priam's Treasure ignited a seductive rush to find lost artifacts mentioned in ancient texts, especially those marked with intriguing monetary value. Undoubtedly inspired by Schliemann's work on some level, adventurers James Lockwood and Robert Marx opened the world of archaeological treasure hunters to an entirely new, previously unexplored realm of discovery, incorporating various land excavation techniques underwater with scuba gear.

Lockwood pioneered early underwater film equipment and helped push sport scuba into the mainstream with several of his inventions. Marx is now credited for numerous underwater archaeological discoveries previously a faint blip on global radar. A new world opened up when Marx located Manila and Spanish galleons, uncovered ancient Mayan temple sites, and spearheaded underwater dive explorations of nearly forgotten Mayan Cenotes.

The ability to find ancient cities and artifacts buried deep beneath the cresting seas pioneered a new frontier for scientific discovery, one which would prove to be as bountiful as the ocean itself to some decree. Restoration of lost human cultures, every artifact a piece of a puzzle truly valued beyond any monetary sum for the priceless heritage it returned.

Renown undersea explorers Lee Spence and Mel Fisher built upon the work of Marx and Lockwood however, shocking the world with rare sunken relics of historic significance that are extremely valuable treasures by material composition. Fisher and Spence were so successful at sea adventuring they managed to rediscover lost galleons worth over four-hundred million at the dawn of sea exploration, burrowing their way into the imaginations of people world-wide.

News headlines of this magnitude inspired many people to become overnight treasure hunters clambering at an opportunity to discover fortune for themselves. Gold fever spreads to the masses quickly, especially with staggering monetary value at stake.

Precious metals, jewelry, gemstones, and other rarities were an integral part of old-world trading, abundant in their cache concentrations. In modern times, commodities are prized for their materialistic value, rarity, and importantly, the history behind each piece. The use of rare elements to define value of commodities may stay around for centuries to come, as mankind's fascination with gold and jewels stems back to the days precious metals were first discovered.

Rare treasures are desired for their captivating beauty, their relationship to wealth, and for the tantalizing tales sometimes attributed to the piece, as the last known surviving memorabilia of predominant historical figures or events. Finding these treasures is to restore lost or forgotten antique craftsmanship once coveted by kings and queens as motivational currencies fueling vast kingdoms and empires throughout the ages.

As with any scientific discipline, advancement of technology allows researchers and underwater adventurers to reclaim history in ways previously unimaginable, though recovering ancient sunken treasures is an arduous task even with modern world innovations. Imagine the effort involved many hundreds of years ago!

Salvage operations then were carried out without scuba equipment, without GPS mapping devices or sonar, and a lack of many comfort amenities found on ships today. Crews faced great risks by depending on free diver recovery efforts amongst sharks to hook cargo for manual hoisting aboard a rescue vessel. As technology improved, explorers faced dangers of diving bells and consequently often used slaves to retrieve items given the bell's high mortality rate.

Underwater recovery was slow, arduous, and at times inhumane. Over time, inventions and innovations effectively changed the process, presenting far less danger to achieve the same objective. Brawn, blood, and sweat turned to ingenious solutions with technology.

Beyond dangerously intensive manual labor driving technological innovations, treasure reclaimers faced privateers and pirates who were just as eager to partake in treasure hunting. Pirates notoriously picked off salvage operations as easy, identifiable prey. To a pirate, sailing into a recovery operation eliminated some of the guesswork, knowing something valuable must reside below if salvage crews were risking their necks diving for it.

As much as reclamation teams attempted to disguise the fact, or find ways to distract scavengers, the inevitable pirate onslaught would drive them away if not successful in a timely manor. Unfortunately in modern times, like in the old-world, pirates still exist by running covert operations. They dive on protected wreck sites and look for ways around maritime treasure laws to facilitate their own greed. A bounty of irreplaceable heritage is lost to black markets routinely when this happens, and along with it we lose an intimate knowledge of our ancestors that may not otherwise be told.

The
Caribbean and Sargasso Seas

Europe's discovery of a new world, far to the west across the Atlantic Ocean, brought about many new opportunities, and some with unforgiving consequence. Uncharted waters and land never set foot upon by European men became a centralized focus. Feuds over the land and its riches quickly escalated between foreign nations and native populations.

The Caribbean and Sargasso Seas are one of the most well-known areas in the world to find lost treasures. A new era in human history began as Spain discovered a provocative endless bounty of the Caribbean; and from here, settlers could conveniently run expeditions into North and

South America. When news broke shockingly across Europe on Spain's return, several inspired countries followed the path, and it was just a short amount of time before serious conflict between foreign reigns would strike the Caribbean region.

Countries courageously fought to wit's end for a piece of this paradise for their own. Beautiful, warm weather, tropical sustenance, and gold attracted kingdoms and empires with a shining promise of prosperity. Much of the area was inhabited solely by native populations, some who were even willing to share with foreign explorers.

For the indigenous people, however, arrival of Eastern countries in search of wealth and land meant the eventual destruction of entire civilizations and vast amounts of knowledge. Precious metals and gems were pillaged in the process, funneled to trading posts, and loaded on ships for transport back to home lands. Foreign expeditions were business ventures aiming to prove kingdoms could expand to the west and profit.

Weather in the Caribbean also has a say in the matter as an uncontrollable dynamic that present danger to any treasure ship in the region. Low pressure systems moving west from the African coast mix with warm Caribbean waters to create tropical storms and cyclones. These storms tend to travel north, up to the Sargasso Sea, above the

Bermuda archipelago.

Spanish expeditions charted trade routes paralleling island coastlines throughout the Sargasso and Caribbean Seas. In the years to follow, these trade routes ultimately crossed paths with strong tropical weather systems, subjecting entire fleets to their wrath. Even the most astute buccaneers were tested to the limits by hurricanes and unpredictable seas.

Colonizing the west presented several new challenges for European countries to overcome. Sailors with an uncanny rebellious nature were liberated by conquering territories and securing large amounts of wealth. Prosperity, privateers, and pirates were born through these new world expeditions, and hostile weather, a routine part of the deal.

Lost Treasure of Cortes

The year is 1504 and a young Hernan Cortes steps foot in the Spanish Santo Domingo colony where he was to became a notary of Azua de Compostela. In this position he contributed to the conquest of Hispaniola, and then onward to conquest Cuba by directive of the crown. With new territory secured, Cortes was placed into a role as clerk of the treasurer and eventually became mayor of the capital of Cuba. By 1518, Hernan found a promising opportunity to explore

Mexico's mainland, but the proposed command charter was revoked by the governor of Cuba, Diego Velázquez de Cuéllar. Appalled by the governor's decision, Cortes defiantly ignored orders, gathered a small army and made way to the Yucatan Peninsula.

In 1519, after repeated attempts to meet with the ruler of the Aztec Empire, Moctezuma, Cortes proceeded to march on Tenochtitlán to confront him. Along the way he gathered allies from the Tlaxcalteca and burned the city of Cholua as an intimidation tactic. The Aztecs however, instead welcomed the Spanish army peacefully into Tenochtitlán believing they were emissaries of Quetzalcoatl.

Gifts of gold, silver, and jewels were given to the Spanish, but unfortunately for the Aztecs, conquistadors interpreted this to be a more lucrative expedition than previously imagined. This must have been a dream come true for Cortes; traveling all the way to Tenochtitlán after no word from Moctezuma, thinking battle would be imminent, only to find the Aztecs presenting him with wealth. Perhaps Cortes believed it as too good to be true.

As conquistador, interests of Spain heavily influenced decisions, and Cortes began devising plans to conquer the Aztec city of Tenochtitlán knowing ultimately the scenario would likely not work out peacefully to Spanish benefit. During the same time, some Aztecs were not happy with Spanish presence in the city. Civil unrest spread throughout and by 1520 the situation escalated to the point Moctezuma was killed.

Rebellion broke out, pitting Aztecs against Aztec rebels and the Spanish. Amidst chaos, Cortes plundered as much as possible and fled back to Tlaxcala. It is commonly believed a majority of the Aztec treasure was lost during this escape due to several causeways connecting the fortification of Tenochtitlán to the mainland. Where this treasure truly ended up is indeed a mystery. Six months after Cortes escaped, an all-out siege on Tenochtitlán begun.

A crippled Aztec empire now faced a Spanish army bolstered by allies and men from Cuba. Any treasure brought back from the previous escape surely aided motivation for the attack by corroborating details of the event, coupled with loss of soldiers during the rebellion outbreak. Siege of Tenochtitlán lead to its downfall and from then on became known as Mexico City in honor of Cortes Yet, the Spanish were unable to recover the gold, silver, and gems.

Covering the city from wall to wall, they searched relentlessly, and only fragments of treasure were found, but perhaps this was the reality. After all, nobody from Spanish conquests openly reported seeing where the remaining wealth was hidden, or for that matter, any cache at all. Hence a tiring search combing the city, as gifts from the initial visit implied much more existed.

However, even though the Spanish did not originally locate a treasure cache during the first visit, or find it after Tenochtitlán's siege, a fair amount of gold, silver, and gems were seized from other locations. It seems likely the huge Aztec city would boast equally or beyond, especially as evident from those offerings the Spanish did receive. Thus, treasure hunters first scoured for known treasure, the plundered riches lost along causeways, unfortunately without much luck.

Draining of Lake Texcoco, a body of water surrounding Tenochtitlán started around 1630 after excess flooding continued to plague the city, and even then the infamous treasure could not be located. Theories suggest the Aztecs recovered the wealth lost in the causeways before the Spanish returned, added it back to their cache, then fled the city in exodus with the valuables. From this point, the hunt turns to many dead ends. Then, a chance discovery in 1992 might explain why.

Off the coast of Florida a shipwreck is found, identified as one of Cortes commission, with an approximate value of five hundred million in treasure. Chests of emeralds, jewelry, ceremonial jade artifacts, Aztec and Mayan relics, and crystal skulls believed to be artifacts from none other than, Moctezuma's rule.

An unbelievable 964 carat gem, known as the emerald of judgment, alone estimated at sixty one million was part of the discovery. Precious jewelry on the wreck dates from the sixteenth to eighteenth centuries, suggesting it was the lost Tenochtitlán treasure. The cache's composition may also be an accumulation from numerous conquests on the Aztecs and Mayans.

According to one account, no hidden or lost treasure in Mexico City could be found after years of tireless searching. Explorers were consistently unable to relocate any gold ditched in causeways, or anywhere in the city area as claimed in legends. Aztec relics discovered aboard the shipwreck may have contained a few pieces Cortes slipped away with during the rebel outbreak, though a substantial amount appears to be from other sources.

However, we understand Tenochtitlán as the equivalent of a modern day metropolis, and an ancient city likely to house an accumulation of treasure from multiple sources. If the shipwreck from Cortes commission transported a different cache entirely, and treasure hunters haven't been able to locate gold in the area, then where did it eventually end up?

A Mixed Armada

The year is 1715 and new tactics for moving wealth are being employed to evade pirates lurking around the Caribbean now more than ever. Previously, Spanish ships making port in the area would run on a regular basis moving sums of gold, silver, gems, and supplies.

Pirate attacks put a halt to the voyages for nearly three years before the Spanish decided these accumulated riches needed to be transported. A plan was put in place, to have several ships fill their holds at ports in Vera Cruz and Cartegena, then have those fleets meet in Havana with a well-armed escort. The armada combined two fleets, one commanded by Don Juan Esteban de Ubilla and the other by Don Antonio de Echeverz. Along for the voyage, Capitaine Antoine Dare commanding a French merchant ship.

Around seven days after departure, the armada approached darkening skies swirling along the outskirts of a strong hurricane. Gusting winds managed to split the group apart, sweeping ships back toward land. At first the winds were a blessing, blowing the boats away from the hurricane instead of directly into it.

However, coral reefs hiding below swelling tides closer to shore hooked up the fleet and they would sail no more. Fortunately for the crew many lives were spared considering more severe possible outcomes. To an unfortunate dismay of the Spanish crown, though, an economy impacting wealth rests on the sea floor instead of in empire coffers.

Salvaging was a long, grueling process, and estimates state only about half of the bounty is eventually recovered. Free-diving the wrecks put workers in a vulnerable position and their visible activity acted as a flashing beacon to pirate opportunists passing by. As word traveled around, pirate pressure escalated. Spain would battle both swelling seas and savvy pirates over a three to four year period to an eventual breaking point; fending off looting scavengers became routine for a while until more notorious pirates made their presence known.

A privateer to become Spanish nemesis, Henry Jennings, put his pirate skills to the test and made off with three hundred and fifty-thousand pesos in his first recorded act of piracy. Salvage operations were forced to retreat due to this confrontation. Eventually pirate activity around the sunken treasure heightened to the point Spain was forced to leave the site, leaving behind a significant amount gold on the sea floor. A conservative estimate values treasure of the entire fleet at right around seven million pieces of eight, or approximately one hundred and twelve million on today's market.

More than half of the mixed armada vessels have been located since the Spanish decided to abandon recovery efforts. The Nuestra Senora de la Regla, Santo Cristo de San Roman, Nuestra Senora del Carmen, Nuestra Señora de La Popa, Nuestra Senora del Rosario, Urca de Lima, Senora de las Nieves, and the French Grifon have been accounted for.

Ships still missing from the armada include the Maria Galante, El Senor San Miguel, El Cievro, and Nuestra Senora de la Concepción. Of these remaining wrecks yet to be found are two speedy carrack vessels that would be more likely utilized for carrying plundered treasures from the new world. In a run-in with pirates or privateers, a carrack stood a better chance of escaping before heavily damaged by cannon fire.

One lost carrack is the El Senor San Miguel, a twenty-two cannon rescue ship that mysteriously vanished during the hurricane with no surviving crew. Researchers suggest El Senor San Miguel was loaded mostly with tobacco when it went down. However, the ship made port in Havana over the winter of 1714 and spring of 1715 awaiting the arrival of the second fleet from Vera Cruz. During this time, the cargo hold may have been reconfigured to include additional goods before leaving for Spain. Perhaps it is possible this was an intended strategy for further protection, by masking the location of riches within a fleet of ships, and the Miguel loaded with plunder secretively.

Part of the fleet treasure was recovered in the 1960's by Kip Wagner after he found a Spanish peso de ocho, or piece of eight, washed up on a Sebastian Inlet Florida beach. Naturally the discovery motivated Wagner, and a mass of new treasure hunters to look for more. After Kip found more silver dollars in the area, an all-out recovery effort began, eventually uncovering seven lost ships along with a significant amount of treasure.

Thanks to Kip it is estimated nearly eighty percent of the armada fleet treasure is now back on dry land, and in museums for public display. Recovering the gold hasn't deterred undersea explorers however. Future discovery of four remaining ships could be very lucrative, especially considering Spain's urgency to have this wealth transported in dire economical times.

Recent finds uncovered two carrack ships which exhibit characteristics strongly resembling other wrecks from the 1715 fleet. The twist, however, it appears they may have been disguised as transporting commodities and mixed cargo while secretly protecting valuable assets. It's definitely a plausible concept considering the Spanish accumulated three years of riches prior to disembarking, including several last minute stores.

Alternatively, the evidence may point to hidden stashes mixed with cargo belonging to ship captains and crew members who routinely attempted to covertly smuggle goods from Spanish government. In either case, smuggled treasure, or intentionally hidden wealth at request of the government, the theory indicates more than twenty percent of the fleet's spoils still resides somewhere beneath the waves.

Revenge of Queen Anne

The year is 1714, and an English privateer by the name of Benjamin Hornigold initiated what is to become an immense pirate republic based in the Bahamas. It's believed the principle motivation for Hornigold's actions during this period is a result of religious consequence, from a controversial changing of family houses on the English throne. Benjamin's longstanding loyalty to the crown, a reason he fought proudly as a privateer, tested to a breaking point.

The controversy stems from the events after Queen Anne of England died, leaving her

Catholic following distraught over the throne's new succession. The Act of Settlement, passed over a decade earlier, now prohibited Catholics from inheriting the crown. Queen Anne's closest living non-Catholic relative is George Louis, a Protestant from Germany. Transition of power in this manor did not bode well for proclaimed Catholic, Hornigold, and his buccaneering career turned quickly from privateer to pirate, reflecting feelings of betrayal by England.

Hornigold's pirate republic started on a small scale by attacking merchant ships using native Indian dugout canoes. Wealth accumulated from pillaging over time and buccaneers looking for their own payback were eager to join his crew. Now with increased resources, and men to fight alongside, Hornigold bolstered the republic in dangerous ways that enabled bands of pirates to hoist black sails together and take on much larger, heavily armed targets.

In the year 1717, Hornigold commandeered La Concorde de Nantes, a slave transport frigate previously plundered from the English by the French and added it to his arsenal. At this time Benjamin took command over a lethal warship named Ranger, which he equipped with enough cannon power to capture or destroy almost any ship in its path. With command of the Ranger, Hornigold makes a decision that would forever change the course of pirate lore. Hornigold appointed his second in command, Edward Teach, captain of La Concorde de Nantes.

Edward renamed the French frigate to Queen Anne's Revenge, likely with a personal agenda in mind. The death of Queen Anne resulting in loss of Catholic rule over Britain must have fueled Edward's ambition to avenge this loss, especially under influence of Benjamin's beliefs. Both Hornigold and Teach now captained their own crews as part of the pirate republic's rapid expansion.

They split off to increase effectiveness and rally larger crowds of pirates. The captains evidently preferred targeting French ships, though a few accounts do mention minor incursions with Spanish vessels. It is quite possible the Spanish were not a primary focus due to delayed news of Spain's alliance with France reaching the captains in time during the Queen Anne's war.

Teach retrofitted his prized Queen Anne's Revenge with enough salvaged artillery to effectively command plunder missions and sailed into the Caribbean looking for new pirate opportunities. Hornigold also attempted to explore for new missions, but his master plan backfired. He commanded his pirate crews to leave British ships alone as a defense should Britain catch and arrest them for pirating.

A poorly thought-out strategy, only employed to protect Benjamin himself, stoked too much animosity between the captain and his crew. Hornigold's pirates revolted, finally tired sitting back, watching wealthy British ships slip by unhindered. Near the end of 1717, Benjamin's crew formed a mutiny to overthrow the captain.

By the time of Hornigold's downfall, Edward Teach assumes his well-known nickname of Blackbeard the Pirate, for his merciless pillaging and plundering of merchant vessels voyaging between Africa and the Caribbean. Blackbeard now resides at the helm of a pirate armada with the combined fire power of more than fifty guns and the frightful audacity of almost two hundred pirates.

Estimations by the year 1718, Blackbeard's crew totaled at least three hundred and fifty men strong according to two eye witness accounts, and the number of ships in fleet vary from two to five from similar reports. An integral part of Blackbeard's strategy is to keep sailing at all times, always a step ahead of merchant vessels, and unlike his predecessor, British targets were not off limits.

Theory suggests Blackbeard employed a unique scouting strategy by sending single sloops ahead, or into a predetermined positions, to signal the fleet from a distance. This strategy tricked victims into thinking a much larger fleet is present, such as an armada that employed several scouts for positioning and lookout. Ships who spot the sloops may get the impression of being boxed-in

Daily plundering activity, though quite successful for a few years leveraging innovative techniques, is about to take a sudden downturn at the height of a pirate republic era. Now the Royal Navy and large privateer fleets are closing in, seeking to end to piracy once and for all with promising pardons for those who surrender. A few pirates did surrender, but it is quite understandable why many viewed promises to pardon pirate crimes with skepticism.

For reasons not entirely or fully understood, in 1718 the Queen Anne's Revenge and a flotilla ship called the Adventure ran aground in the Beaufort Inlet shallows off the coast of North Carolina. The incident is controversial as whether or not grounding was an intentional careen, perhaps for the sake of crew members or for Blackbeard himself; a mutually beneficial solution for Teach to abandon his pirates and ditch the Queen Anne's Revenge, to find a ship less-identifiable by the Royal Navy.

Blackbeard's pirates removed anything valuable from the wrecks, right down to metal hinges, divvied it up and left the boats behind to face the crushing blue. The flotilla accumulated an undisclosed amount of wealth over the years and this plunder is believed to be aboard at the time of grounding.

Personal loot of Blackbeard, gathered during the time of dugout boat attacks might have been part of the plunder as well. With pirates leaving their ships behind and taking any valuables with, it explains why artifacts of significant value are rarely discovered during dives on the wrecks. The ships were picked clean and now the question, where exactly is the treasure?

Treasure hunters researching the whereabouts of Blackbeard's elusive cache stumbled across local legends claiming the notorious pirate frequented caves around the British Virgin Islands and the Black Bay area of St. Lucia since the time of his first act of piracy. The legend continues by noting Blackbeard hid treasure in these caves for later retrieval, a common pirate act of the era.

Similarly, the same legend applies to his loot from the Queen Anne's Revenge, suggesting part of this treasure was ditched in caves also to be retrieved later. Without doubt, true a pirate of Blackbeard's ability to devise a plan, retaining plunder should he escape a seemingly inevitable date with English gallows.

Torres Hurricane

Unfavorable weather in the Caribbean tests the ability and skill level of any ship captains, especially as conditions sometimes develop into super storm cells producing violent winds, damaging ocean swells, tropical storms, typhoons, and hurricanes. Combination of rising tides and strong winds present unforeseen dangers to even the largest of ships and most savvy captains.

Storms in the open seas are capable of flooding holds with excess water from abnormally high waves cresting above the deck at a moment's notice. Rogue waves coupled with dangerous winds can easily capsize a ship or set it off-course unknowingly into rocky outcrops or shoals lurking beneath shallow waters. Limited visibility from dense rain and fog along with low-light or night conditions only increase the risk of disaster.

Sailing the open oceans relies heavily on weather conditions, from wind affecting momentum to undulating currents adjusting course. Aside from human error or intervention, the weather is a major factor in determining a successful voyage. While reading through shipwreck stories it becomes apparent just how dangerous weather can be for ship captains. If weather isn't directly attributed as the cause of shipping disaster, it becomes the most likely culprit until otherwise proven through underwater wreck explorations; to the point shipwrecks and bad weather become nearly synonymous.

Foul seafaring conditions echoing those from eighteen years prior, to the misfortune of General Torres and Spain, demonstrates how devastating weather affects shipping operations within a moment's notice. A strong hurricane managed to wipe out an entire Spanish fleet in 1733 as they attempted to quickly traverse dangerous waters transporting large amounts of treasure. The armada consisted of four heavily armed galleons, and at least seventeen merchant vessels laden with gold, silver, gems, and other precious cargo.

Words of Don Alonso de Herrera, one of the surviving captains, recounts the unfortunate tragedy in a detailed message to Spanish authorities. Researchers gain valuable insight into a monstrosity the fleet faced, this being the second time in close succession that a large Spanish treasure fleet met with the gruesome ferocity of a hurricane, leaving only survivors to tell the story.

Alonso describes sailing into the knife's edge of a hurricane near the Florida Keys that presented very little warning. In a desperate attempt for survival, the armada grounded intentionally in the shallows to wait out the storm. High winds gusted toward the fleet upon meeting the leading edge. Untrimmed sails were clipped and masts twisted as seas churned.

Swelling tides, reckless white caps, and ocean sprays flying in every direction. The fleet's fate quickly sucked into the danger with high winds and waves prohibiting escape toward Havana. Everything happened so fast that by the time captains attempted counter measures, many ships we're already too saturated to stay afloat.

Grounding the ships proved to be the next logical decision for survival. A grounded vessel keeps it mostly upright and helps deter capsizing while providing shelter for the crew, and in such, hunkering down saved lives.

When the hurricane finally hit, only a few of the ships were actually destroyed by direct impact, while the remainder were stabilized enough to prevent imminent disaster. It is uncertain exactly who commanded the first orders for intentional grounding, though some research indicates Alonso most likely made the call. The decision became a blessing in disguise for Spain, not only considering an alternative outcome, but also because the shallows were close enough to land for survivors to establish temporary camps and recover supplies from the wrecks.

Proximity to the shoreline allowed salvage crews to work quickly off-loading while keeping an eye on the goods. In fear of pirates happening upon an eighty mile stretch of grounded Spanish treasure, crew members burned any ship debris above the waterline to hide evidence in lapping waves.

Divers worked diligently pulling up any valuables they could find. In as little as three months of hard work, to the pleasure of Spain, every piece of registered treasure recovered. Beyond this news, salvages also managed to recover a large amount of unregistered valuables from the site. Effectively, the Spanish recovered the entire fleet's wealth, and also a significant amount of treasure being smuggled away from the crown.

In modern times, both private and commercial salvage operations have attempted to recover additional treasure from the grounded fleet without much luck. Spanish salvage operations were so successful that little remains to be found on the sunken ships, a true testament to Spain's claim of recovering the entire wealth. Even the best known preserved wreck yielded very little bounty worth the time and effort for salvage.

Today, one wreck from the 1733 fleet, the San Pedro, remains as an underwater archaeological preserve and diving attraction. The dive site also serves as a thoughtful reminder that hundreds of years ago, an astute Spanish captain found a way to save the crews and treasure of twenty two ships from a powerful hurricane.

Tucker's Missing Cross

One of the earliest known treasure shipwrecks disappeared from existence for nearly three hundred and fifty years, sunk in a shallow just off the coast of Bermuda, right on the doorstep of commercial deep sea fishing trawler traffic. Famed treasure hunter and underwater explorer, Teddy Tucker, discovered what he believed to be the San Pedro, an early 1594 Spanish ship christened to honor St. Peter.

Though several Spanish ships assumed the name of St. Peter throughout the course of history, this particular San Pedro is famously known in underwater archaeology as one of the first major treasure recoveries from modern times. Among the treasure found on the San Pedro is a single, delicate, and mesmerizing piece made of gold and emeralds that would forever change marine archeology along with the world's perception of underwater treasure hunting.

Sifting through historical records to find the origin of Tucker's prize discovery ship proves difficult. At the time of operation, San Pedro was a fairly common name to be associated with a seafaring vessel. However, the records narrow possibility to three predominant ships adorned by the name St. Peter sailing at the time of, and near the area of the ship Tucker found.

When examining the routine sixteenth century Portuguese and Spanish fleet operations, four Atlantic-bound routes tend to stick out as the most feasible explanations. The routes outline return trips toward either Azores, Lisbon, or Seville, from either Veracruz, Havana, Portobelo, or Cartagena. These are documented trading ports linking the Caribbean seas to Spain by proximity of Bermuda. Stops at Cartagena or Portobelo may have also included layover port in Havana on the return, depending on the nature of the mission.

From this information, two ships from the narrowed list may be eliminated as unlikely due to both time and location. First is the San Pedro captained on a course in the complete opposite direction, by famed explorer Sebastian Rodriguez Cermeño. Sebastian followed a trade route in the same year from Acapulco, Mexico to Manila, Philippines across the Pacific.

The second ship crossed off is openly, and mistakenly, attributed as Tucker's discovery ship, San Pedro captained by Hieronimo de Porras. Interestingly, the Porras St. Pedro did follow a similar route along the coast of Bermuda, but at a different time. Porras is officially recorded as leaving the year after Tucker's prized wreck is first reported missing.

With two ships eliminated by time and place, the third known possibility is a curious vessel most likely to be the identity of Tucker's mystery ship. This San Pedro sailed from Spain in 1594, the same year as Bermudian historians officially date the wreck, and it followed an exact return trade route passing through Bermuda's coastal waters.

Record indicates the third San Pedro was captained by Pedro Nunez de Bohorquez who sailed under protection of an armada en-route to Portobelo from Spain. The armada's plan intended to have Nunez split off toward Rio de la Hacha, or Cartagena, to load up and continue on its journey back to Spain.

After raising anchor in Cartagena, the Nunez San Pedro then followed the return trade route heading north ahead of its armada, hooking around Havana, then out across the Atlantic toward Azores while carrying respectable amounts of treasure in the hold.

Historians determined the ship met its fate in a dangerous section of the Bermuda coral reefs known as the Isles of Devils. Almost a hundred years prior to San Pedro's sinking, this area was often visited as a rest stop along the way to Caribbean trading ports, but a combination of bad weather and eerie animal noises at night turned the archipelago into a freaky legend, with warning to avoid at all costs.

Although the ship likely sailed in the vicinity of Isles of Devils, exactly how San Pedro sunk remains a mystery to researchers. However the tragic event took place, one thing is for sure, the wreck spent a few hundred years peacefully on the ocean floor, lost and forgotten until a chance discovery in 1955 by Teddy Tucker.

On a routine salvaging mission to recover lost commercial fishing equipment, Tucker happened upon San Pedro's artifacts accidentally. While searching the ocean floor for a large fishing net, he noticed the faint glimmer of dark metal in the sand. Upon a closer inspection, the metal turned out to be multiple bronze cannons, and a few were recovered at the time with scrap dollars in mind.

Tucker marked the site to find it easily again then proceeded to find a buyer. The Bermuda Monuments Trust Commission presented a considerable payment well above any offerings from salvage yards before Tucker had a chance to scrap the cannons. Of course this success immediately prompted Tucker to return to the site.

The return visit in 1959 would ignite Tucker's career as a full-time underwater explorer, and at the same time, rock the foundation of modern treasure hunting. On this dive, Tucker uncovered an immaculate gold cross encrusted with seven stunning emeralds, the same cross later featured in Bermuda's 1969 commemorative collection.

The initial cannon discovery ultimately lead to a highly successful and lucrative salvage operation, and the beautiful ornate cross became an object of affection. Treasure hunters and collectors from around the world are drawn to its craftsmanship and value. Admirably, historical importance of this discovery was understood by Teddy, and he donated the cross to Bermuda's Aquarium Museum for it to be treasured by thousands for years to come.

Tucker's donation catches public attention. Value of the cross quickly escalates and antiquities collectors around the world suddenly become much more interested in the cross. Perhaps some collectors were even willing to go as far as necessary, to procure the piece for their own.

Then, a sophisticated and well-executed heist reminiscent of capers shaking the art world during the period, replaces the Tucker cross with a nearly exact replica despite protection efforts of Bermudian authorities. Government officials are lead to believe the swap must have been an inside job, and years of investigation failed to locate any solid evidence. Over fifty years after the incident, the whereabouts of the authentic treasure's location, and who was responsible for its disappearance, still remains a mystery.

As intricately stunning and beautiful as the cross is, this isn't the only of its kind to be found on sunken treasure ships. For example, another renown undersea explorer by the name of Mel Fisher recovered a memorizing twenty-two carat emerald cross from the 1622 wreck of the Nuestra Senora de Atocha, strikingly similar in design as the Tucker cross.

The Atocha, like San Pedro, followed a trading route ultimately destined for Spain after visiting the Cartagena region of the Caribbean. Similar cross designs other than Fisher and Tucker's, vary in overall size with five to seven beautifully square and round-cut style emeralds set into finely sculpted gold cross pendants, finished with elaborate decorative detailing.

On a few sunken treasure recovery operations, similar styled jewelry is discovered within the captain's quarters, including a gem-studded cross with a thick full necklace chain stashed away in an exquisitely carved ornate gold keepsake box. Given the design complexity, level of detail and location found, these decorated crosses seem to present their own royal sense of mystery capable of captivating anyone who lays eyes upon them.

Ships of a Gold Rush

Discovery of gold in the western United States changed the country on multiple levels and shaped the way people perceived the west coast. Instead of a distant and mysterious area seldom visited by Easterners at the time, California became known as a place of prosperity and hope capable of forever changing lives and families.

Although gold non-ferrous, it still possesses a unique magnetic quality of attracting people to its source. This is especially evident with the California Gold Rush, when many thousands of prospectors from all over the continent literally rushed west in the late 1840's searching for new found wealth and treasures.

Aspiring treasure seekers wasted as little time as possible to find their way to mining claims. The journey westward encompassed the idea of any means necessary, from wagon trails, horseback, and passenger ships. Those heading west to the land of new prosperity managed to overcome harsh conditions associated with the journey only then to be subjected to rigors of a wild mining frontier. Gold fever found a comfortable place to settle in western America as thoughts of striking it rich overnight filled the minds of men across the continent.

Success of the first prospectors who landed in California in 1848 quickly grabbed news media attention. Mass migration swept the land by 1849, after multiple headline stories proclaimed lucrative discoveries of gold in California, and as much as fifty million worth pumped into the economy each year during the rush.

With over hundred-thousand people migrating each year, the hundred and forty day wagon trips were too slow to keep pace with demand and faster routes were reasonably desired. The majority of adventurers chose to travel over a much shorter time period on forty day paddle-wheel steamer routes with a short land jaunt at the end.

Steamships became a preferred method for reaching the west coast and also provided a means for establishing infrastructure which would connect the relatively unexplored west with business operations in the east. Although steamships are attributed for transporting the majority of folk to California during the gold rush, traditional sail powered ships were still largely in operation and carried many thousands in their own right. Sail, steam, and hybrid powered ships traveled along the east coast around Florida and through the Gulf of Mexico to Panama capitalizing on the opportunity.

The land pass from Panama across Central America involved dangers of trekking through dense jungle, but it remained the quickest route provided a ship was available to take passengers up the west coast upon arrival. Trouble taking the land shortcut is one reason why some ships decided to skip the Panama pass altogether with a route heading around South America, crossing Cape Horn, and then back up the west coast to San Francisco. Prospectors could reach San Francisco in thirty to ninety days via this route provided there were no complications though Cape Horn or run-ins with pirates along the way.

During the rush, gold in California was ever abundant, and many prospectors found fortunes of a lifetime in the hills, but what happened to the gold extracted at the time? We know part of it stayed in California to be minted, and also, a portion used for trade amongst prospectors and proprietors to keep operations running. The remaining treasure, to a historical understanding, traveled to New York for minting in Philadelphia with a portion traveling to London, England for processing.

Gold valuables retrieved from California moved home with prospectors or direct to processing facilities by way of contract workers on return trips. Those returning often traveled from San Francisco to Panama City, then crossed to board a ship en-route to New York. Many prospectors likely reveled in their new-found wealth on the return voyage, and probably kept an ever watchful eye on their caches throughout the long journey back to New York.

In the fall of 1857, a cargo transport side-wheel steamship aptly named SS Central America, and its crew of one hundred followed a most regular routine; securing thirty-thousand pounds of California gold along with almost five hundred passengers returning to New York.

Patrons considered this a favorable time to travel, and excitement on the steamer must have created a wonderfully pleasant atmosphere to travel by. With only a few short hours remaining in the trip, the atmosphere on-board was about to change. The steamship approached the coast of South Carolina, right into the path of a category two hurricane.

The storm swooped around, trapping the SS Central America in high winds and rough seas. Gales ripped the sails apart and sprayed large amounts of water off swelling wave crests on deck. The spray and crashing waves became too much for the steamer to handle, the ship's holds were soon overflowing, and threat of sinking is now very real. Excess water in the holds snuffed out the boiler, and without sails to push away with, the Central America was sucked deeper into the storm.

Captain William Lewis Herndon and a dis-traught crew in full-fledged emergency protocol, fighting desperately for the lives of hundreds of people. Among the chaos, the ship's flag hangs upside down acting as a distress beacon, eerily symbolic of the steamer's inevitable fate.

Able passengers and crew frantically worked through the night bailing water, trying to get the boiler running once again, and to save everyone from disaster. Almost a day into distress efforts, a small West Indian brig by the name of Marine met up with the SS Central America with some much needed relief.

By this time, chances of restarting the boiler were next to impossible, and the outcome became all too apparent, the SS Central America had reached the rope's end. In a noble act, Herndon personally helped evacuate over one hundred and fifty women and children onto the Marine, packing it beyond capacity. He then waited on the Central America with his crew and remaining passengers for future rescue.

Agonizing hours passed with no sign of help, not a hope in the distance. Water continued filling the holds far too quickly to compete with, and time ran out. SS Central America along with its captain, crew, four hundred passengers, and thirty-thousand pounds of California gold sunk to the sea floor. As news reached home, families and loved ones of returning prospectors were absolutely devastated.

A developing American economy depending on wealth from the gold rush was also affected by the significant loss. It's theorized this tragedy contributed on some level to the Panic of 1857, the first world-wide economic crisis. With no way to find or recover the SS Central America, it unfortunately became forgotten and lost on the ocean floor.

Nearly a century and a half later, the crushing,

heartfelt story of the noble Captain Herndon, and lost wealth from the California Gold Rush, would resurface into public media once again. In 1987, the wreck of the SS Central America was discovered off the coast of South Carolina at a depth of seventy-two hundred feet, incredibly far deeper than previously imagined.

To this day, recovery operations with modern technologies have salvaged roughly twelve-thousand pounds of gold so far, to a sum of almost hundred and fifty million dollars worth. The remaining Gold Rush treasure, some eighteen-thousand pounds, slightly over three-hundred million worth, has not been located.

A Captain's Lost Fortune

A considerable number of researchers and fans of pirate lore tend to associate Captain William Kidd as without doubt, one of the worst pirates in history. William's mark on the pirate world is one too often presumed as fueled by illogical decision, yet there are a handful of researchers who believe Kidd's reign to instead be calculated and cunning.

Some of those unsavory decisions placed Kidd in an unsettling position and he spent the latter part of his privateer career attempting to restore

England's faith in his actions. William however did not fall short in catching targets off-guard, or in presenting alliances with unexpected and sometimes unorthodox methods for obtaining bounty. This paints a very different picture of Captain Kidd, instead as a master savvy sailor who's secrets attribute to success beyond common measures of privateering wit.

During the 1690's, Captain William worked for authorities, commissioned by governing politic in New York, and Massachusetts, to apprehend and deter pirates tormenting merchant vessels crossing the Indian Ocean. These delicate operations were exceptionally risky, yet the discerning privateer swiftly brought about justice all the while bordering lines of maritime law. Kidd knew the rules intimately and adhered to code in a prudish effort often met with scrutiny by authorities. Treading on a toxic line between privateer and pirate is sure to test any man's allegiance over time, and the edgy captain would soon find this out first hand.

William's swift actions against piracy placed him among ranks of sailors also willing to balance on that fine line with maritime law. Maintaining a good standing offered protection with reward, and for Kidd this was plenty of incentive to keep to code. However, one questionable event would alter England's perception of the edgy privateer, indicating his allegiance seemed to be faltering.

The event, though rather amusing in hindsight, gave the crown further reason to scrutinize. William and his crew intentionally failed to salute the Royal Navy as custom dictates upon passing vessels. Instead of a typical salute of respect for the crown, the rowdy bunch of would-be pirates dropped their drawers and mooned the Royal Navy as they floated by. This didn't sit too kindly with subjected officers, and news of the defiant incident soon reached England.

On top of making a bold statement to the crown, this news also gained audience with a few unruly pirate fellows, including Captain, Robert Culliford, the pirate who once commandeered one of Kidd's ships. Further eyewitness reports investigating Kidd outlined problematic abuse and blatant torturing of prisoners. These reports were also intercepted by pirate captains on their way to English command.

When England received word of William's latest fiascoes, the Royal Navy identified with a pre-emptive label of pirate since the actions did not officially warrant trial. It appeared now, in the eyes of the Navy, that Kidd's loyal ambitions to England were breaking. Kidd is now viewed by the law as corrupt over his associations with pirates, and perhaps, rum-drunken with power bestowed to uphold English law.

For the time-being, Kidd and his crew continued privateer missions commissioned by the crown. England, with reason to distrust, paid much closer attention to the escalating situation, still with no hard evidence capable of bringing Kidd to trial.

William found himself a way off the plank after a suspicious attack on a Mughal convoy; which is now identified as Kidd's first act of piracy. He somehow reasoned as extenuating circumstances significant enough for England not to pursue. Then, as it would seem, a final tipping point pushed the borderline privateer to full-fledged pirate once and for all, presenting England with fair right to have Kidd stand trial.

A short time after a questionable Mughal attack, Kidd confronted an Armenian ship sailing under French colors, named the Quedagh Merchant. The vessel appeared to be fair game for privateer commendation, but then William later discovered during capture that the ship's captain was an Englishman granted privilege to sail under French protection.

At this moment Kidd attempted reasoning with his crew to let the French ship free, and to leave its sailors unharmed. The cargo holds full of gold, silver, and prized silks enticed the unsavory men, and the crew decided there will be no such accord. When the pirates refused to give up the loot, Captain Kidd decides to side with them.

William is now officially on record with England as a pirate.

After scuffling over the Quedagh Merchant's loot, Kidd's rowdy pirate crew commandeered and renamed it, the Adventure Prize. Years following the capture take their toll on Kidd and it becomes apparent the action was a haunting one. William fought his urge to restore good standing with England, but it continued to grow much stronger.

Kidd proclaimed his innocence to the crown, stating the Quedagh Merchant and previous incidents were entirely fortuitous, but England no longer trusted him. The privateer now turned remorseful pirate struggled to continue, laden with guilt instead of treasure, and success of operations began to dwindle. The crew grew irritated at the lack of prosperity and received little or no payment for their efforts.

Finally, during a pirate hunt off the coast of Madagascar met William face to face with facts of an unsatisfied crew waiting for an opportune moment. While surveying ship activity, Kidd spotted none other than pirate captain Culliford, the man who made away with one of the ex-privateer's ships earlier.

William planned an attack on the unsuspecting pirate captain Culliford. The enervated crew cast doubt on Kidd's motive with belief the ambush to be revengeful rather than a serious reward. Disgruntled at the captain's plans, Kidd's crew instead became mutinous and abandoned him on the spot to join the likes of Culliford.

Together with Culliford's men, the mutineers proceeded to remove everything of value from the Adventure Prize, and then turned their sights to a second ship called the Adventure Galley. They stripped all remains of treasure and metals, right down to door hinges and irons with a burning desire to leave William with nothing.

After valuables were secured, and the Adventure Galley left in ruin, Culliford and Kidd's former crew sealed its fate. Kidd pleaded in a traditional pirate bargain for a share of loot before being left stranded. Robert and his men agreed to the accord. Also fortunate for Kidd, thirteen of his men did not mutiny and elected to continue on with him. Next stop, New York.

As a wanted pirate for actions against Quedagh Merchant, William could not simply sail directly to New York without crossing paths with the Royal Navy. Countering this, he set sail towards the Caribbean in a final effort for freedom. To escape England's prosecution, Kidd first sought to evade it.

Knowing the former French ship, Adventure

Prize, would easily be detected by the Navy, he stashed it in a lagoon on Isla Catalina and gave the remaining thirteen men permission to barter off cargo should lucrative deals persuasively present themselves. After making arrangements for the Adventure Prize, Kidd offered a portion of saved treasure for a sloop named St. Antonio, and with this he could sail under cover.

William made off to New York, believing the accusations of piracy would be pardoned and seen as purely accidental. According to records, Captain Kidd thought additional leverage may be necessary and may have stashed treasure along the way to be used for bargaining should the need arise.

Finally, upon arrival, Captain Kidd did not have a chance to plea for pardon. He was arrested on the spot and thrown into the brig, the plan backfired. Kidd's years of loyal service to the crown did not absolve his actions, even if truly fortuitous by the claims. It appeared this was the end of the line for the remorseful captain. Then, in 1701, England made an example of Kidd, sealing his fate. The crown's actions were a loud, eerie warning to all pirates, as William hanged on the shoreline in an elevated iron cage until death. After which, he remained on public display for three years.

Given the nature in how he died, it is uncertain

to this day whether or not Kidd's leverage came into play during imprisonment, or at any time before the hanging irons. Stories about his treasure became legends mixed with details of a controversial privateering and pirate lifestyle.

In 2007, true to legend, the Adventure Prize is found off the southeastern coast of Catalina Island, presumably untouched by wreck looters since its sinking. According to documentation, the thirteen men left to barter became impatient awaiting Captain Kidd's return in 1699 and pillaged the ship before sending it to the sandy sea floor set ablaze.

Quedagh Merchant was discovered by Indiana University's diving science team before it could be scavenged by modern treasure bandits. The team found twenty-six cannons, three functional anchors, and metal objects indicative of a scrap iron heap believed to have been left in the hold; all matching historical record.

Gold, silver, gems, or any valuable treasures associated with the captain were not discovered, further corroborating details of the ship's final moments. Adventure Prize now resides where divers first discovered it, protected for future generations to enjoy on recreational dives.

Furthermore, legends speak of a treasure map left behind that designates where William buried his bartering cache along the way to New York. The described map does exist, though it is yet to be proven authentic. Shreds of evidence suggest a distinct possibility it might be genuine, which has inspired modern treasure seekers to continue the hunt.

However, there an oddly strange component on Kidd's treasure map; The location points at the Cape Verde islands off Africa's western coast. It's reasonable to consider William would pursue great lengths to protect his leverage, but is it possible he sailed the small St. Antonio sloop to Africa and back before heading to New York?

Perhaps the sloop wasn't involved at all when the map was created, suggesting that William hid his cache near Cape Verde while on the way to the Caribbean from Madagascar. Stories told regarding the Culliford confrontation do not mention a side trip to Cape Verde, or intentions of Kidd to stash some of the treasure. If this were the case, then the thirteen men who chose to continue sailing with William undoubtedly knew about it, and they probably attempted to return to the location after sinking the Adventure Prize.

Margarita and the Atocha

After Spanish conquistadors seized control over Inca settlements in Peru, necessity for moving vast resources increased dramatically along with an inherent risk of doing so. Small, privateer commissioned fleets intended to capitalize on treasure shipments while demonstrating loyalty to the crown. Spain bolstered flota presence by sending large galleon warships to protect and defend merchant vessels.

At the peak of new world expeditions, Spanish fleets reached upward of eighty to ninety ships systematically composed of two or more heavily armed treasure galleons, merchant, supply, and communication boats. Strategically positioned armada convoys offer greater protection from smaller pirate fleets and modest defense against malevolent bandits.

In 1622, an armada of twenty-eight ships strong assembled in Havana to haul a shipment of wealth to Spain from recent expeditions. Within the fleet are two heavily armed galleons, the Santa Margarita and Nuestra Senora de Atocha, designated to transport the bulk of spoils. After experiencing a few delays at port, the two galleons were then packed to the brim with copper, silver, gold, gems, and an assortment of prized handcrafted jewelry.

While loading the Margarita and Atocha, crews fortified a war fleet to accompany the two laden galleons, acting a heavily armed protective cover. Merchant ships traveling with the armada also provide a type of distraction from treasure ships, and in their own right, taking advantage of the war fleet presence to safeguard trade goods such as tobacco and indigo along for the trip. Once assembled, the fleet raised anchor from Havana on a fair day with a great start toward a promising sail. Crews kept a watchful eye for pirates, suspicious activity, and foul weather that might compromise the mission.

Unbeknown to the armada, a storm system brewing just beyond the spotter's horizon would soon push the sailors to their limits. Hurricane force winds sweeping the area pushed the armada off course and into shallows just past the Dry Tortugas region. Coral reefs obscured by churning waters ripped through fleet hulls, sinking the majority.

Reports indicate upwards of six-hundred people died or went missing during the fast-moving incident, and the crown suffered dearly from the loss of both lives and wealth. Spain returned to the scene shortly thereafter to salvage wrecks, only to find debris trails were scattered even further, as though a second hurricane placed the final nails. Violent winds had recklessly tossed ship debris along a fifty mile trail.

Loss of an entire flota and new world treasures distressed Spain, and it would be a long, difficult, setback to recover from. Adding to this, timing couldn't have been worse, right in the middle of European war. Spain's only choice to continue funding sieges during the Thirty-Year's Palatinate, to sell galleons they would've used otherwise for retrieving western treasures.

Spanish salvaging recovered generous portions of treasure from Santa Margarita, but the Our Lady of the Atocha evaded discovery for over three-hundred and sixty years. Then in 1985, five years after recovering pieces of the Margarita, world famous undersea explorer Mel Fisher located the Atocha seventy miles off Florida's coast near the Marquesas Keys.

Despite the fact Atocha met with two hurricanes before sinking, Fisher believed he found the majority of treasure intact as it was lost hundreds of years prior. Mel uncovered a cache of Gold, silver, gems, and precious artifacts totaling well over four-hundred million on today's market. Among the valuables from the Atocha were two items prized for their beauty and rarity; an exquisite twenty-two carat emerald cross, and a mesmerizing emerald ring.

With both treasure galleons discovered and picked clean, focus shifts now to the remaining fleet. Could there be additional treasure aboard those ships? Circumstances of the fleet's demise have made it challenging, even with modern technology at hand, to locate where the remaining ships are residing. We know Spain recovered a portion of the treasure off Santa Margarita, and Mel Fisher salvaged a significant portion of the Atocha riches, yet records suggest the potential of finding much more. The two galleons may have held most of the fleet's loot, however, Spain spent a considerable amount of time and funds in attempt to fully recover all that was lost.

Operations narrowed in on the Margarita for

nearly ten years with side efforts on the Atocha and merchant ships until Spain was eventually forced to cut the loss. This suggests the Spanish government knew much more treasure was onboard at the time of sinking, possibly even more than what Fisher uncovered hundreds of years later.

Several survivor reports from the Atocha and Margarita's last moments describe the smaller merchant vessels sinking within a visible range. Wealth aboard merchant ships may have been severely underestimated by modern researchers, well beyond the indigo and tobacco indicated in cargo manifests.

One reason for the discrepancy is noted by frequent occurrences of treasure smuggling during Spain's expeditions. Precious metals and gems were hidden from the crown to avoid taxes. The 1733 fleet disaster which occurred years later is a great example of this practice, with Spain recovering excess amounts of wealth slipping past detection of authorities.

Another explanation for the existence of additional treasure is in fact due to overloading. Namely, the possibility Spain could not fit all of the treasures aboard the two galleons, and may have been split it between merchant vessels. With pressure mounting on the Spanish economy for war efforts, officials may have elected to transport loot beyond ship capacities. Under either circumstance, finally locating the remaining ships will help determine this once and for all.

Morgan's Treasures

By the end of the seventeenth century, privateer operations reached a pinnacle and account for the capture of many thousands of ships on behalf of government payment. The profession boasted lucrative returns greater than mediocre wages usually offered to navy sailors, but with the promise of large rewards lurked a substantial amount of danger. Greater reward often presented a greater risk in dealings with pirates.

Privateers act on their own accord within the confines of respected governing houses, for armistice, commission, and similar perks offered poignantly to detain those at war against, or in cahoots with the crown. Beyond funding for privateering, these entrepreneurs were commonly presented with additional ways to generate income, and along with this, a viperous temptation for piracy.

Proven success privateering gained audience with governments and more lucrative opportunities presented themselves. Welsh privateer Henry Morgan, for instance, gained authority from Britain to launch full scale attacks on Spain after establishing a notorious presence in the Caribbean with large privateer fleets.

As part of his bargain, Morgan kept generous portions of any seized treasure while the English crown wins with victory over Spain, making him a very wealthy man by the time he retired from privateering. In fact, estimations place Henry's net worth at retirement upwards of fourteen million in modern equivalent, a substantial feat considering the daily risk involved in the profession.

Morgan's treasures accumulated slowly at first as he worked his way into a commanding position over several ambitious years. His notably unrivaled loyalty to the English crown was clearly demonstrated early on by an eager willingness to fight for territory, even if it meant sailing a fair distances with minimal knowledge to participate in battle. The entrepreneur's valor and determination earned a position of captain under command of Christopher Myngs, a stepping stone which would become the very foundation of Morgan's privateering fleets.

The Spanish considered Christopher a pirate with foul intentions and as a commander who would stop at nothing to bring about destruction and murder. Lord Windsor, the English governor of Jamaica at the time, helped Commodore Myngs establish a massive fleet capable of carrying out plans to destroy Spanish settlements in the area.

Fourteen-hundred buccaneers sailing on fourteen ships dedicated to ransack and pillage the Spanish, and among them, the fearless Captain Morgan in an opportune position with access to a powerful arsenal. Unorthodox methods utilized by both Lord Windsor and Christopher Myngs eventually stirred a great deal of controversy with the English government.

On multiple occasions, Myngs and Windsor defied requests from the English, blatantly refusing to stop pirates from pillaging Spanish ships. England and Spain were on the verge of reaching a treaty during territorial conflict, and in light of this, England began attempting to help protect Spain in a show of good faith. Lack of help from Lord Windsor subsequently prompted his replacement with Thomas Modyford, who in 1664 became the new governor of Jamaica.

Modyford also found trouble in defending Spanish vessels from pirates and continued to issue attacks on Spanish ships and settlements. At the height of delegations, England requested all privateers and pirates to cease operations against the Spanish they reached a peace agreement, yet privateers and pirates did not halt. Instead, they continued to plunder under Modyford, who then placed Henry Morgan in a more predominant role of command.

Morgan is now poised to take the Caribbean by storm, and with several letters of marque from Modyford authorizing all-out siege on Spanish, Morgan spared no delay. Henry quickly attacked Puerto Principe, gaining around fifty-thousand Spanish pesos despite a tip-off warning Principe of the impending attack. After this, ransack on Portobelo net approximately two-hundred thousand Spanish pesos.

Then, Morgan and his men sailed to Cartagena seeking the vast wealth cache at the well-fortified garrison of Cartagena de Indias. It was in Cartagena where Morgan commandeered a French vessel he accused of piracy against the English government. Legends also suggest the possibility Morgan secured a significant amount of treasure from the Spanish at this time although historical record doesn't seem to record the plunder.

Cartagena, located on the south-western edge of the Caribbean Sea, is an important Spanish trading port during the seventeenth century also known as Rio de la Hacha. The post collected gold, silver, and gems obtained from expeditions to Peru and New Granada, and funneled these riches onto galleons for sailing to Havana. Spain's treasure fleets often traveled from the Cartagena region transporting large amounts of wealth. Some theories suggest the lost treasure of Hernan Cortes was recovered by Spain and sent to Cartagena, and that Morgan managed to obtain it before retiring in Jamaica. For this to be possible, the treasure of Cortes must have unlikely stayed in Cartagena port for well over one-hundred and fifty years.

The key to Morgan's success as a privateer who retired wealthy, is attributed to his ability to siege entire Spanish settlements and their ships, yet credit must also be placed with Modyford for enabling the situation to ignite. Modyford trusted Morgan's ability and continuously provided the authorization Morgan needed to perpetuate plundering.

Henry stood for England and believed strongly in converting new world colonies into English, even if it meant treading dangerous waters and testing patience of the crown. Morgan was truly a fearless, savvy buccaneer capable of launching attacks even after deflation from a previous defeat.

His predecessors helped him build the largest known privateering fleet of the time and from this Morgan learned to command successfully.

The
Chilean and Scotia Seas

Treacherous waters surround the southern most tip of South America, where it is claimed the ocean is at its most unforgiving. Trade ships were forced around Cape Horn for hundreds of years until the Panama Canal offered a short-cut. To reach the far east, vessels often sailed the eastern South American coast before crossing the Pacific. This was a head-on approach with a shorter trip compared to looping around Africa, across the Indian ocean and south China seas, but the dangers made it very risky.

Ships braving a trip around Cape Horn face a powerful Antarctic Circumpolar Current, combined with williwaw and prevailing winds along the Drake Passage. Traveling through the Strait of Magellan in Chile reduced danger enough for more reliable trips to Peru, Malaysia, and even San Francisco during the gold rush.

A large number of ships have disappeared around Cape Horn due to the severe weather, ice bergs, monstrous waves, and sudden gale-force winds. These are normal, day to day occurrences around the southern edge of South America. Facing a storm system in the Drake Passage becomes that much more life-threatening.

The imminent risks of sailing around Cape Horn also make the area very difficult to explore underwater, let alone attempt to salvage treasure from a wreck below. Chances of recovering a lost ship sunken deep in the fast moving Antarctic Circumpolar Current are slim, and it will take specialized technological advances to change this in the future. However, diving the Strait of Magellan or the hundreds of canals between islands at the South American tip is far less dangerous, and many shipwrecks are safely accessible with the right equipment and determination.

Despite the unimaginable dangers of sailing around Cape Horn, many explorers were also successful in reaching new territories on the west coast of South America, the Galapagos biological treasure trove, and many previously uncharted Pacific islands. Without bold captains, rugged crews, and exceptional navigators, this part of the world may have taken hundreds of additional years to become accessible by boat.

Lost Gold of Lima and Pisco

In the mid 1800's, a modest and reportedly humble church located on the coast of Peru became the unfortunate victim of a dastardly scheme appropriately reminiscent of pirate legend. The Pisco Church filled its large coffers with what would prove to be a dangerous amount of treasure over the years from various Spanish expeditions. During the time, churches often served a secondary purpose as temporary storehouses for excess treasure and safe-guards were put in place to protect the wealth. Stores at Pisco however, took on a little more treasure than originally intended due to its centralized location in Lima.

To protect the church's cache, guards were on duty around the clock, keeping a watchful eye for anything threatening. The bulging coffers caught attention of four devious men who then worked up a scheme designed essentially, to simply walk off with the treasure. In the elaborate setup, the men attended the church on a regular basis to establish trust with the ministry.

Eventually they were in a position to help guard what would soon become their loot. Then, according to plan, a diversion was set to draw the church's attention away from the cache which conveniently left the men alone to stand guard unsupervised. Without delay, the men quickly plundered the church and fled from the scene.

Exactly how much treasure the men made away with is unknown. Some frame of reference exists which describes the church cache in its entirety according to recorded losses, and report details from the ministry, but this is the closest to accurate valuation known.

Estimations from those accounts suggest around fourteen tons of gold were potentially on site at the time of plundering; around five-hundred and thirty-six million on today's market in metal value alone. Along with the gold were two valuable chests containing precious goods organized for safekeeping. One chest held an estimated five hundred-thousand in Spanish doubloons, and another full of premium quality raw gemstones. Topping the treasure off, ornate gem-encrusted crucifixes and candlesticks adorning the church, also plundered.

Four men devised a plan, which according to legend succeeded in moving a substantially wealthy cache from the Pisco Church, however, curious questions cast serious doubts over the logistics of such a feat. Fourteen tons of gold would require a method of transportation, perhaps horse-drawn carts in succession, for moving the treasure without too much suspicion.

How the men were able to accomplish this depends a lot on how the loot was stored at the church and what tools the men readily had access to. For example, if Spain kept the treasure on rolling carts, a detail not mentioned in legends, then the scenario becomes much more plausible.

After plundering, the four men chartered a ship to Australia with a plan to ditch the treasure along the way before arriving then return for it later. Popular legend indicates the ship stopped at lush atolls nestled in the mid-Pacific where the loot was stashed at the bottom of an island pool.

Which island pool?

Four locations are mentioned as potential hiding places including Pinaki, Katiu, Makemo, and Tahiti in the French Polynesia. These locations are well-known and part of a reputable sized series of beautiful atolls dotting the ocean between Peru and Australia. Several lesser known islands are easily in vicinity of the aforementioned which adds difficulty to decipher exactly where the hiding took place.

Adding to the mystery, the kicker, all four men were killed before they had a chance to return to the hiding spot. This is one of many versions of how the legend explains the last known location of Lima's treasure. Researchers discovered the story of treasure plundered from a Pisco church has surfaced over the years in several eerily similar versions. In fact, the legend is likely to be a derivative rooted from a famed mystery, the Loot of Lima, reported to take place at least thirty years before Pisco church event.

There are slight variations between the legends, but the overall essence remains; that a large amount of treasure with similar composition was plundered from the coast of Peru and buried on an island somewhere out in the Pacific or on the way to Mexico. By similar composition, the earlier mystery also describes gem-encrusted crucifixes, candlesticks, gems, and a cache of gold.

Though, the major discrepancy between the Pisco church legend and the Loot of Lima mystery is the amount valued to have gone missing. In the earlier event, an estimated sum of sixty million in gold went missing from Lima. Could it be both legends are the same story told differently, that the Pisco legend is an exaggerated version of the Loot of Lima?

Spain's exploration in the area, and a necessity for stockpiling treasure at various staging sites, this significantly simple question is also perplexing to a point. Generous amounts of precious goods were accumulated during conquests, so much in fact, that filling multiple churches and storehouses became part of due process.

Pisco is close enough to Lima for relatively short travel by sea or land over two-hundred and forty kilometers, and both locations have persuasive reasons why a large cache of gold, gems, and jewelry would be stored on site. Along with this, treasure may have moved between these two locations for protection during the height of regional conflict.

Both legends feature a number of similarities possibly indicating the stories are born from the same event. In each, the treasure's composition is described as gem-encrusted candlesticks, ornate crucifixes, and a measurable amount of gold ornaments thieved from a Spanish church. Lima's legend roots from an earlier time and references a much smaller treasure in comparison to Pisco, yet both legends identify the robbery as an inside job. Perhaps in this consideration, the two legends demonstrate an alternative explanation, that the same men were involved in pillaging both churches or word of their success inspired copycat heists.

The event at Lima claims wealth accumulated by the Catholic church is scurried north by ship to Mexico for supposed protection prior to civil outbreak. Captain Will Thompson devised a scheme on the journey north to retain the treasure for himself and managed to eliminate the crew. Thompson then transported his spoils to Cocos Island for burial and later retrieval.

Interesting enough, the Pisco treasure faced a similar fate years after this incident. In the Pisco legend, four men obtain a church's riches which they haul off to sea and stash it for later retrieval. Both legends leave the treasure's whereabouts in question, buried somewhere on a remote island in the Pacific.

Lima became a hotbed for loot storage during Spanish prospecting in the region, and it's quite possible enough treasure existed in both locations to account for each legend, suggesting instead both are plausible and not derivative. The composition at each location is likely to be very similar, that is, if the wealth stored originated from a much larger source before it was split between storage locations.

The
East Asian Seas

In the sixteenth and seventeenth centuries, expeditions around the world picked up the pace to an inspirational level, seeking to find land, resources, and new cultures to trade goods with. At this time, a large portion of the Earth was mapped with an impressive degree of accuracy; though there were still many unexplored regions. Cartographers detailed shapes of Africa, South America, Asia, Malaysia, and North America, that greatly improved world navigation by ship.

Progression through the mapped world leads to an understanding that North America and the Arctic were a single land mass, as well as Australia and Antarctica. Finely detailed coastlines were usually those frequented by exploration efforts and often leveraged in trade operations. One region demonstrating this impeccable detail examines the coastlines of Malaysia, Philippines, Papua

New Guinea, and the Southern China seas.

Exploration of East Asian seas revolutionized the world by opening up methods of trading and discovery. In fact, it is the amped exploration of East Asian seas and the Indian Ocean responsible for initiating the historical Age of Discovery. Water-bound expeditions cascaded even further around the planet thanks to flourishing trade in the East and a necessity to expand into new territories.

The northern land route, known as the Silk Road, connected China to major trading hubs in India, Persia, and the Mediterranean. Precious goods and spices flowed across the Asian continent for thousands of years until Ottoman and Byzantine conflict forced merchants to find an alternate route. To compare with the Silk Road success, the route needed to be capable of crossing thousands of miles without interference.

Shipping routes in the south seas were long established, moving cargo between the Red Sea, India, and Malaysia. Success of these sea routes attracted Silk Road merchants as an alternative way to reach destinations without having to worry about the Ottoman and other resistances. The spice trade now flowed mostly unhindered, crossing oceans instead of land, and consequentially it created a boom in Eastern trade.

Traveling by the East Asian Seas enabled spice traders to easily reach cultures in Malaysia and southern passage to India, Africa, Egypt, Arabia, or Red Sea without having to extend the Silk Road further and further north. Eventually, by the ninth century, prosperous sea routes expanded around Africa, up to Europe, and across to South America. From busy outposts in Lisbon, Seville, and Antwerp, trading extended across the Atlantic into the Caribbean Seas with some return routes crossing the Pacific to Manila on different ships.

European discovery of North America, by inspiration of East Asian exploration, opened an entirely new realm of possibility. Hundreds of trade ships sail the globe by the early sixteen century, and spice traders made this possible. Eventhough wars broke out between nations, and significant amounts of cultural heritage were lost, societies from around the world adapted and shared knowledge from foreign lands which helped to set a foundation for a cultural melting pot named North America.

Legend of Yamashita's Plunder

The story of Yamashita is one that is a little different from traditional pirate lore, not only because it's set in a more recent era, but also by the scope and complexity of the Yamashita operation. In the early twentieth century, Japan faced crisis as poverty struck the nation, plunging the economy into one of dire straights.

To combat this, literally, Japan took arms sending thousands of troops to sweep across China, pillaging and plundering everything in their path.

From banks to school houses, Japanese forces participated in a ruthless endeavor to restore wealth of their own country with seemingly no remorse. This became a dark period in Japan's history, stealing for the survival of the country.

Gold, silver, jewelry, and other precious items obtained were moved back to the coast, then shipped back to Japan using a staging ground in Bacuit Bay, Philippines. The forwarding post acted as a repository, whereby ships could make continuous runs to and from China faster, then transport the plunder to Japan afterward. According to some researchers, though, ships were moving wealth back to Japan the entire time, and that the repository area held very little in terms of the war effort.

Stories have become modern legend implying otherwise, and this is where controversy ensues. As with the height of the war, Japanese forces were backed into a mountainous corner and spread across the Philippines. According to locals who accompany their stories with detailed treasure maps, the Japanese buried plunder from China in over one-hundred and seventy hidden cache sites around the Philippines.

Legend claims Japan became so burdened by war efforts that ships transporting stolen treasures could no longer be fueled, prompting wealth to be left at this staging site. These legends incidentally spawned a cottage industry in the Philippines, whereby locals offer to take tourists on excursions in search of buried treasure. Every local involved claims to know exactly where the treasure is, and yet, requires payment for their services.

Questions beyond this are raised regarding other parts of the legend's logic, asking why Japan chose to distribute the stolen treasure in caverns and bury it in mountainsides. This would be an effort far beyond necessity in the time of war, especially when they lost control of shipping routes and could no longer fuel. Why not, perhaps, keep the plunder at one or two guarded sites for its eventual transport after the war, why expend even more resources to hide it?

Another theory suggests a smarter strategy, to move the treasure to neighboring countries such as Taiwan, or leave some of it controlled in southern China. No records indicate exactly where the spoils ended up, and it's a reasonable expectation to believe Japan was capable of using diverting tactics to protect the plunder.

Perhaps in that, activities in the Philippines were a small part of a much more complex plan. One in which details were carefully leaked out to locals along with bold action to create a facade, misdirecting focus during the war effort far away from the loot's true journey. Researchers are aware gold has been discovered on the island, but they're largely unsure whether or not the gold found was salted.

What were thought to be significant discoveries in modern times turned out to be hoaxes designed to keep this cottage industry generating money years after the war. For example, a large cache of bars were found with a very small percentage of real gold, leading investigators to believe the treasure was planted by local profiteers. From this it is understood the truth of where Yamashita's gold went may never be known despite years of searching by both professional and amateur treasure hunters.

Massive Fleet with No Return

China's great Ming Dynasty revolutionized its people and state by working toward stabilization of resources and sustainable farming. During this period, eunuchs, though outcast or positioned as slaves in some circles, were trusted with more power in others.

Their castration often resulted in poor social treatment by some, but it also lead to higher levels of trust from emperors, as privy to listen to, and relay messages of political significance on their behalf. From this, favored eunuchs found themselves in more powerful commands with interest to the emperor. In the early fifteenth century, the Yongle emperor entrusted a eunuch, Zheng He, to spearhead one of the largest exploration missions in China's history.

With help from the Yongle empire, massive armadas were constructed with wooden ships so large they would dwarf all others and ultimately face the limitations of floating wood vessels. Zheng commanded what he deemed, Xiafan Guanjun, a fleet capable of literally transporting a city of soldiers, workers, and horses. The size of the armada reached nearly thirty-thousand sailors by the height of exploration missions, something difficult to achieve even in modern times.

Around sixty two, nine-mast Boachaun treasure ships composed the fleet's core, surrounded by over a hundred and eighty support ships. The support ships were composted of eight-mast Machuan horse ships, seven-mast Liangchaun grain ships, six-mast Zuochaun troop ships, five-mast Zhanchuan warships, small rowing patrol and water tanker boats.

Xiafan Guanjun followed ancient trading routes on diplomatic missions, procuring sumali qin cobalt used in the production of imperial blue and white porcelain. They sailed on seven prominent voyages from Nanjing off the eastern coast of China, to Sumatra, around the Bay of Bengal, the west India coast, following Arabia into the Red Sea, then along north eastern African coast.

Zheng's armada also searched for gifts and novelty for the empire while promoting Ming's power with a daunting array of ships.

The fleet was absolutely massive, and in many respects, intimidating as intended. Historical documents give us an idea of just how large Zheng's ships were, and for years archaeologists considered the numbers to be slightly exaggerated. That is, until the discovery of a thirty-six foot rudder in 1957, then two more similar lengths in 2004, at ancient shipyards in Nanjing.

A few calculations confirm, that a ship utilizing a rudder this long is estimated to be over four-hundred and twenty feet long. Rudder size at first coincides with four deck Boachauns by proportion. The ship yard itself, however, reveals possible evidence of even larger, seven deck Boachauns were constructed during the same period.

An often debated mystery remains to this day, whether or not Zheng He's ships were actually as large as recorded documents indicate. Wreck sites which would help provide this necessary evidence have not been discovered. What we do know is after the seventh voyage, and despite demonstrated navel success to Chinese court, Xiafan Guanjun was abandoned as the empire sought to align resources elsewhere. Multiple theories have surfaced regarding the fleet's whereabouts and there are no known incidents leading to ship sinking or casualty on a scale as large as the fleet.

Partial evidence suggests the armada was left abandoned in harbor after its discontinuation. Furthermore, it may be possible by some accounts that Xiafan Guanjun had been intentionally burned. A considerable amount of resource and wealth of the empire made it possible to float the fleet, but perhaps obtaining cobalt and other reagents we're not enough to offset costs.

South China Seas

As diverse as the world's cultures, so to are treasures from past generations hundreds and thousands of years old. Priceless ornate artworks record cultural heritage in a variety of forms through talents of extremely gifted artisans. Subtle details decorating each piece are clues to archaeologists, demonstrating a period and place craftsman spent long hours to perfect their artwork.

Artwork from China for example, features specific elements requested by ruling emperors, allowing researchers to essentially pinpoint the time and place it was created to a very accurate window. This is especially the case as historians race to recover, catalog, and preserve several ships once lost in the treacherous waters around Malaysia.

Merchant vessels dating back as far as the fourteen century, that wrecked in the Melaka straights, have been discovered with barge-sized shipments of white and blue porcelain pieces, over thirty ships in all. A few merchants were also transporting a number of ornately decorated urns, metalworking ingots, ivory, timber, and green tea along with small payloads of porcelain.

The route, although dangerous in some areas, was a predominant trading hub in the fifteenth and sixteen centuries with both Chinese and Dutch East Indies ships making port on a regular basis. As discovered from wrecked ships here, Sisatchanalai and Sukhothai were both large porcelain production sites. Prior to studying these ships in particular, scholars understood that Sisatchanalai was a major producer, but now Sukhothai's major product role becomes much more clear.

Among treasure discovered throughout Melaka straights wreck sites are rare, well-preserved porcelain dishes, plates, and teapots dating between 1368 to 1644 during the Ming Dynasty.

Then there were six consignment pieces with markings of Emperor Xuande dating between 1424 and 1436 from the Ming Dynasty. Another pleasant surprise demonstrates the continuation of trade activity in the area throughout many hundreds of years, with rare Yixing teapots dating between 1821 to 1850 found aboard a ship by name of Desaru.

Another ship, by the name of Diana contained over twenty-four thousand precious blue and white China porcelain dishes. Nanyang, a Chinese merchant ship found in the straights carried large urns decorated in Sisatchanalai patterns among a generous selection of ceramic pots, bowls and earthenware. Yet another significant find came from a secret compartment on the Royal Nanhai, with a consignment of five ornate blue and white ceramic bowls, ivory sword handles and the minister's stamp.

Rare, high quality artisan porcelain fetches hefty prices on the collector's market, which has unfortunately triggered mass thieving off wreck sites. Ships posing as fishing trawlers drag nets over the sunken boats in attempt to dredge up some of the treasure. At what price though? This type of operation not only destroys the site from being preserved for future generations to enjoy, but it also literally trashes heritage that may not otherwise be restored.

Certain collector items, like a prized chicken cup known for exquisite quality and signature artwork, recently fetched upwards of fifty million at recent auctions due to overwhelming rarity and demand. It is a similar demand driving pillaging of ceramics from many ships in the Melaka straights. Stores have popped up on the Internet offering the chance of expanding private collections with rare pieces, and this type of behavior prevents museums from sharing a country's heritage with the public.

Peking Man and Awa Maru

Treasure lost aboard sunken ships tends to be irreplaceable and this, along with the treasure's story, adds to its value whether monetary or priceless. Famous treasure finds that manage to capture the world's attention are often ornate crafted gold and jewelry attached to legends which demonstrate an empire's wealth and power.

At times, however, the lost treasure is far more rare and valued by world heritage than any precious metal or gem. One example of this in particular are remains of the Peking man presumed missing when a ship sunk during the second world war. The fossils are profound to humanity, dating to anywhere between three-hundred to almost eight hundred-thousand years ago, identified to be part of none other than Homo erectus ancestors. Several attempts to locate and restore the missing artifacts have turned up dry and the Peking man's location is unfortunately still unknown.

Excavated from a historic site near Beijing, China in the late 1920's with further discoveries into the thirties solidified the Peking man's fossil identification. Multiple skulls, teeth, and stone tools found in the area provide a glimpse into the lives of primitive Chinese ancestors. The fossils became a prized treasure of mankind after research studies demonstrated their significance, and were protected just as other valuable treasures of the time.

Resources for many countries in the second world war were spread thin, and as casualty affected more people and supplies it became increasingly necessary to make the most of what resources were available. This ultimately included refitting machinery and ships for war purposes, using them to facilitate the effort for a prolonged period. An infamous passenger ship called the Awa Maru is a testament to the lengths Japan would go at a time when principal resources were running out.

The five-hundred foot long vessel initially built for transporting passengers was quickly transformed not long after completion to haul a large amount of ammunition and reinforcements, then serviced for missions to follow. It fell victim to torpedo attack, underwent structural repairs, and was eventually recommissioned to supply relief in support of Red Cross efforts.

In its second-to-last voyage, the Maru moved a large amount of wealth in gold, silver and platinum to Singapore. With the destination ultimately being Thailand, eyewitness speculations also suggested the Peking man artifacts were part of the same cargo.

The theory describes Awa Maru's last voyage to be escorting a large shipment of precious metals along with the Peking man fossils and a few other invaluable artifacts. In fact, the Chinese government spent multiple millions in recovery efforts to salvage the ship, believing this to be true according to their own records. However, hijacked communications by United States intelligence tells a completely different story. Recordings and transcripts identify Awa Maru off-loading its precious cargo in Singapore well before sinking.

Some eyewitness reports corroborate this fact by describing a lesser valued cargo of rubber and copper aboard the ship as it left Singapore. If the precious cargo was off-loaded before the Maru's last departure then it is likely to believe the Peking fossils were too. China's salvage efforts managed to locate the ship, then reported nothing of value was recovered. This further supports the fact treasure was off-loaded beforehand or that possibly, it was part of a strategic plan.

Another, more accepted theory, traces the missing fossils to a United States Marines ship named the SS President Harrison. Captain Orel Pierson reports detail a journey from Chingwang-tao to Manila transporting several hundred marines and a fourteen-hundred ton cargo. The ship was tracked by Japanese forces and then captured, sending the crew to prison camps and the cargo to an unknown location.

According to record, the Peking man fossils were among cargo confiscated which originally were intended to travel by safe passage from Qin-haungdao to the United States. This is the last known and most credible report to date places the fossils traveling from Peking Union Medical College by rail to port. Meaning, the fossils must have survived port in Singapore aboard the Awa Maru and nearly four-thousand mile journey to Beijing before leaving the college.

The
Arabian Seas

Ancient sea trading routes around the South China Sea, Bay of Bengal, and Malaysia further diversified the Orient by connecting people to new cultures, new ideas, and a vast untapped wealth of knowledge. Merchants traveled by ship to Somalia, Egypt, or Madagascar by crossing the Indian Ocean and Arabian Sea, while transporting silks, spices, and treasures for trade. Scholars learned from foreign cultures firsthand while developing a deeper understanding of the world.

Expeditions into the Gulf of Aden and Red Sea introduced a profitable link to the Mediterranean Sea. Now merchants had an effective way free from the harsh Gobi desert to Greece, Italy, France and Spain conveniently within a sail's reach. Summer monsoon winds carried ships to and from new lands for trade. Camels and riverboats extended sea routes further inland to the Roman Empire with communication and goods from the east.

Trading via the Arabian Sea started much earlier than when it became an extension of the spice trade, in fact many hundreds of years prior to when many Silk Road traders migrated to leveraging sea-based shipping routes. Antiquity describes large Egyptian ships capable of carrying goods as old as 1420 BC, and huge Greek warships, quite able to move trade goods if desired, dating to a time older than the eighth century before common era.

Sailing vessels were common in the Arabian Sea, and occupied the waters on a regular basis thousands of years before Spain traveled to the Caribbean for the first time. A way to envision overall, how active ships were in the Arabian Sea is a view of many trading ports dotting its coastlines. At least fourteen major hubs connected the Arabian and Red Sea coast with active routes stretching from Alexandria to Sri Lanka by the year 250 current era.

Monsoon winds changing directions with the seasons provided breathe at a sail's back across the Arabian Sea. Although some scholars believe it wasn't until the fifteenth century before trade winds adapted their name, sailors crossed the Arabian Sea and Indian Ocean on Northeasterly and Southeasterly trade wind patterns thousands of years beforehand.

Escape Pretoria with Gold

Tales of long-lost treasure are consistently mysterious, intriguing, and enticing. Discovering a fortune in abandoned gold appears to be lucrative, to say, all that has to be done is follow the clues to wealth. Yet, the small important details tend to have trouble budging a seeker's naivety given the stakes.

One such mystery, worth an approximated two-hundred and fifty million in gold coins and bullion, draws treasure hunters around the world year after year. The discovery of the Krugerrand fortune promises both wealth and prestige, but finding it has proved to be more difficult than first perceived.

In 1880, the British Empire challenged South Africa's Transvaal Republic for control over the territory. Under the command of President Paul Kruger, the Green State managed to fend off attacks, to the point British Prime Minister William Gladstone settled in armistice. The cost of war provided little in return for Gladstone to justify sending more men and supplies necessary to overturn the republic. Six years later, however, a massive gold field discovered in Witwatersrand gave the British Empire a new reason to pursue occupation of Transvaal.

This time, however, thousands of British immigrants flocked to Witwatersrand seeking gold, and eventually out-numbered the native population. Aligned with the gold hunters is a growing military military presence on the Transvaal border. The combination of immigrants and militia became concerning to the Transvaal Republic. President Kruger issued an ultimatum to the British stating that if they were to invade in attempt to seize the wealth of Pretoria, every gold coin and bar would be escorted away from the area and hidden from the British. In 1900, Kruger fled as he claimed, taking the gold with him on wagons in fear of the oncoming attack.

Historians researching the event have determined Pretoria's gold was divided into three loads, each traveling on a five-hundred and fifty kilometer route to further evade the British. It's assumed that one of the wagons went through the town of Ermelo and was buried by the British to keep it hidden to be picked up later. Kruger traveled to Europe on a Royal Netherlands Navy cruiser sent by Queen Wilhelmina.

An infamous ship, the HNLMS Gelderland, picked up Kruger from Maputo (Lourenco Marques), now the capital of Mozambique, to make port in Marseille, France near the end of 1900, and then later in 1901 to Indonesia. A cargo manifest for the 1900 Gelderland voyage may shed light on part of the mystery here. Except. If Kruger indeed brought the wealth of Pretoria gold to Europe, it's likely this would be kept secret.

Gelderland traveled to the Dutch East Indies after dropping Kruger in France according to records. Did the Krugerrand gold follow route, being the very reason why it hasn't been found? Or was the treasure secretly split once again and funneled into the East Indies growing infrastructure?

The records indicate Kruger stayed in briefly in Germany, Netherlands, and Switzerland after arriving in France. He attempted to gain assistance from governments to help Pretoria rise above British invasions, but each of the countries elected to not get involved. Statements regarding Kruger's last dealings even suggesting he might have offered gold as evidence of wealth to be had in Transvaal.

Goa with the Spoils

In the early 1500's, Portugal attempted to make contact with the prosperous trading port Sultanate of Malacca at the height of Malay power. Malacca was the Malay capital, a bustling port trading Indian cloth, Chinese porcelain, silk, and spices amassing great wealth in the process.

The Portuguese conquered Goa in 1510 as part of strategic presence in India although it was not initially part of the occupation plan. Those orders targeted Hormuz, Aden and Malacca, but it was from the unauthorized capture of Goa where the Malacca invasion staged. Curiously along on the trip to Malacca, the world famous explorer, Ferdinand Magellan.

Initially the Portuguese did not commence battle on arrival and instead attempted negotiating prisoner release and permission to build fortifications. The assault began quickly after the negotiations failed to produce satisfactory results. Malacca was defeated with Sultan Mahmud Shah fleeing before the invasion could reach him.

With port siege, the Mar filled its hull with an estimated eighty tons of riches, including two-hundred coffers of precious stones, diamonds, gold, silver, copper and tin coins. Also inside the cargo hold were many richly crafted items created for the King and Queen of Malacca.

Afonso de Alboquerque directed a small fleet from Malacca under the command of António de Abreu toward the East in search of the Spice Islands; possibly with Magellan aboard. Afonso and Flor de la Mar set sail toward Goa with the spoils. The weather turned for worse, churning a devastating typhoon in the middle of the night. High winds and waves combined, forcing the captain toward a coastal area.

At this point the vessel ran into a beach, splitting the ship in two, dumping the seized fortune along with expertly crafted priceless Chinese lion statues into shallow churning, sandy waters.

Much of the crew were lost and the wrecked Alboquerque watched as the waves finished his vessel off.

Last known whereabouts of the four-hundred ton carrack place it sunk near the end of 1511, somewhere in the Malacca Strait. A departure date is not recorded, which would help greatly to determine a final resting area. There are plenty of locations at the northern end of the Malacca Strait where the Flor de la Mar could have run aground. Depending on when Afonso left, and the ship's speed, it is possible the tragedy involved the Nicobar Islands while swinging West to Goa.

According to one historical account, some of the Flor de la Mar's fortune flotsam was recovered, but the largest portion of the treasure is still unaccounted for. The theory claims local natives may have salvaged the riches, but this is really only speculation according to other researchers on the subject.

In commentaries of Afonso de Alboquerque, it is stated the only plunder saved was a ruby ring, a golden sword, and a crown. The wreck itself is still awaiting discovery over five-hundred years later. Shifting sediments, tides, and currents have likely played an important role in masking the ship's discovery throughout the ages.

The
Northern Seas

Lost sunken treasure may be found all around the world, even as we look to regions outside of warm tropical zones frequented by merchants and explorers. For thousands of years, routes in the Mediterranean Sea connected Africa to Europe and Asia, allowing Romans and Greeks to trade with Egyptians and eventually reach India. Then, Britannia established a sea route following the coastline from Great Britain through the Strait of Gibraltar, connecting northern lands with the Mediterranean's prosperity.

Viking expeditions found passage to the west, visiting Iceland and Greenland. Archaeological findings indicate around 1000 CE, the Norse established a small settlement on the coast of Newfoundland, Canada. Considering historical importance, L'Anse aux Meadows is a recognized UN-

ESCO site that validates Norwegian presence in North America.

However, the first Norwegian discovery of North America may have been entirely an accident as the sagas also suggest. One saga mentions a merchant named Bjarni who landed on a foreign coast during a trip from Iceland to Greenland. A violent storm blew Bjarni's ship some distance to the south, by the description, to a land rich in trees and hills covered with thick forests.

Over a decade later, the Norse returned to Canada's coast on an expedition mission under the command of Leif Erikson. After landing, Leif named the new land, Vínland. Careful study of the area suggests L'Anse aux Meadows was a staging ground for further expeditions inland. For the time-being, evidence is scarce to prove how much of North America was discovered by the Norse, and it's believed they returned to Greenland after several disputes with natives.

Then, hundreds of years after the Norse visited the Eastern Canadian coast, news of Spain's first successful voyage to a new world spread across Europe like the black plague nearly one-hundred and fifty years earlier. News of Christopher Columbus discovering America created a different kind of pandemic though, and the mad rush to North America begun.

Missing Crown Jewels

Treasure lost to the sands of time may not always succumb to the treacherous fate of violent seas as the land itself may finish the job long before an ocean is given tranquil opportunity. For a treasure to sail the tides, it must have originated on land to meet port bound for a bountiful horizon. This is especially the case with buried loot intentionally stashed in the ground for later retrieval.

Pirate legends notably mention the idea of buried treasure in locked chests along with cryptic maps where X marks the spot. To uncover such finds means many things bestowed upon the seeker, such as riches, power, and even curses. However, in some cases those treasures kept away from prying gold-fevered fingers may be told they rest in the ground, but is this really the truth?

In the year 1214, bad turned to worse for King John Lackland the first of England. Facing the ill fate of excommunication by his most loyal followers, Pope Innocent the third, and feudal barons. King John was forced to sign Magna Carta in 1215 which limited his ability to rule over the people of England.

The Pope supported anyone willing to take the crown which became a great opportunity for King Louis the eighth to complete his occupation of England by seizing the throne. Prince Louis entered England in 1216 and was given homage by King Philip the second of France and the Barons, he was not crowned midst the war. The crown jewels along with a large collection of gold, jewelry, and precious gems accompanied John on a historic campaign of reclamation across England.

According historical accounts, John traveled to Norfolk and then decided to return after falling victim to dysentery. He elected to send his treasure carts along a treacherous route called The Wash, an area only passable during low tide.

Shallow bay areas around the world are known to see rapid inflows and outflows as the tide comes in making it a dangerous place to be. On top of that, The Wash in particular has several deep channels created from rapid tidal outflow. Sudden influx of water across the flats can cause a number of phenomena able to trap men and horses such as whirlpools, strong undertows, and liquefying soil.

A common belief suggests Lackland's horse-drawn treasure carts did not move quickly enough to combat a rising tide and it's possible some men may have become trapped in an outflow channel. Studies of the event suggest sediment build-up over the years eventually buried the treasure up to 20 feet below the silt, making it near impossible to recover, a plausible explanation for why the crown still remains lost today.

One curious part of the tale is the claim several of King John's men were lost along with the horses and carts. This means to treasure hunters, if the lost crown jewels were found, it is very likely complete sets of medieval armor, weapons, and other important artifacts lay nearby also waiting to be discovered. It is estimated the current value of the crown jewels alone is around seventy million.

Norfolk is known as an area where many rivers meet the sea. To frequent Norfolk for a prolonged period privies one to an intimate knowledge of how those rivers may be used to an advantage. Some believe it might be possible King John's trip was part of a larger, more devious plan to plunder the crown treasures for himself while strategically offing the royal guard. This accusation spawns partially from an event rumored to happen between John and his nephew Arthur.

Speculations suggest the King took his nephew out by boat, killed him, and dumped his body into a river. Many attribute the story of Arthur's demise as symbolic of King John's cruelty and ruthlessness. Arthur would interpret the trip as an opportunity for isolation to privately discuss important matters without realizing those private matters meant his own disposal.

The rumor demonstrates John's ability in foresight to execute a diversion, staging waterways to conceal truth and fulfill ulterior motive. From this concept one might ask, how do we know the treasure carts sent across Norfolk bay weren't met with boats at low tide in a secretive master diversion? Or that John instead sent the kingdom's prized possessions on a vessel out of Norfolk beforehand, planning the bay crossing to retain control of the crown jewels?

Those who witnessed the event then perished in the wash while the King escaped, essentially absolving him from anyone pressing to have the jewels returned. This assessment creates more of a conspiracy, giving John credit for devising a master plan to flee from excommunication while retaining riches of the throne.

Lost Klondike Gold

After the great American gold rush took California by storm in 1848, only a short amount of time managed to pass before the frenzy hit once again. This time, however, much further north in areas with far less favorable weather conditions. The Klondike managed to reawaken gold fever, attracting around a hundred-thousand prospectors, of which thirty to forty percent completed the long journey into Alaska; and of those who made it, ten percent found gold.

Those determined to confront harsh conditions in return for the wealth of their dreams followed treacherous land passes through the mountains or paid inflated rates for a ride aboard boats heading up the coast.

A variety of ships put into service capitalized on voyages to the Klondike, and then again on the route back. Conservative estimates value around one billion in gold, on modern markets, traveled out of the Yukon by the passenger ships alone. Three main waterways lead to Dawson City, including a route inland along the Pelly River, the Skagway route just off British Columbia's coast, and the Pacific Ocean meeting with a northern branch of the Yukon River. It was along the Skagway where one prestigious ship, the SS Islander, met with an unfortunate disaster during a 1901 return trip.

According to an article published in the Detroit Free Press, and confirmed by a letter from Canadian Customs Officer E.S. Busby, the Islander hit an iceberg near Douglas and Admiralty Islands. Approximately twenty minutes after the incident, SS Islander started a descent toward the river bottom, carrying with it the lives of around sixty to eighty passengers.

SS Islander is closely associated with many stories of the Klondike gold rush as it brought many to and from a new land of promise reliably, and in modest luxury, up until this point. After the unfortunate event, stories flourished speculating over how much gold went down with the ship.

The Detroit Free Press article notes a sum of two-hundred and seventy-five thousand, while the Canadian Customs Officers mentions a packet of gold dust lost along with cargo, ballast, and stores.

At the time, gold was worth around nineteen dollars per ounce, meaning a bit over fourteen-thousand ounces (nine-hundred and one pounds) were reported on-board at the time. On today's market that equates to a little over seventeen million, however, this estimate does not include a reduction percentage based on impurities eventually to be removed later during refining.

Accounts from some of the survivors suggest between three to six million in dollar value of gold placed on the Islander prior to departure went down with the ship. This larger estimate equates to roughly twenty four million in current market based on inflation, and may be an accurate assessment if considering the potential amount of unregistered gold aboard.

Multiple attempts to salvage the lost Klondike gold have met with little or no reward for the effort. Even a well-thought operation which dragged the ship to shore at Admiralty Island revealed only a small amount of treasure; along with the fact more of the bow was missing than previously imagined. Further correspondence from Canadian Customs revealed the SS Islander's gold was kept in the bow area which broke off completely during the sinking.

An expedition team has located the missing section, and yet, no gold has been recovered from this area of the wreck for the better part of almost twelve decades. Now, this certainly raises an eyebrow and effectively establishes a much deeper mystery with one question. Did the Klondike gold really sink with the SS Islander?

Mercedes Returns to Spain

Escalation in regional conflicts during the heat of Spanish conquests in the late eighteenth and early nineteenth centuries took its toll on Peru. By the year 1800, Peru's population dwindled to one fifth its size as casualty. Spain continued pillaging, all the while shipping as much plunder as possible across the Atlantic in name of the crown, without mercy for lives affected.

Despite efforts to continue, Spain's struggle increased by pressure from Peruvian civil unrest. The peril in Peru devastated millions and in order for the crown to justify its efforts, it became increasingly necessary to transport treasures far away from points of conflict or else jeopardize Spain's successful pillaging.

In 1804, as carried out many times in the past, cargo vessels with sails trimmed to the wind, departed the Caribbean transporting a variety of goods destined for Spain. The weather was mostly favorable and allowed the ships to make decent time without major problems. Traveling together on this voyage were four vessels. The Medea, Clara, Fama along with the famed Mercedes.

On board, a generous cargo obtained from Spain's successes in the region including wool, tin, copper, seal skins, oil, silver dollars, and gold ingots. In fact, the manifest records declared in detail the fleet carried nearly two million silver dollars, one-hundred and fifty-thousand gold ingots, and a silver value of almost one and a half million in remaining cargo.

The ships succeeded in crossing the Atlantic, and were on their final approach to Spain when they met with four British warships in the straight of Gibraltar. The Indefatigable, Medusa, Lively, and the Amphion. Mercedes opened fire across the bow at the British, initiating the battle not long after initial confrontation. Medea somehow managed to escape without pursuit as the British elected to concentrate fire on Mercedes, the instigator as it were.

Clara pleaded no contest, surrendering midst scattering of the Spanish fleet. The Fama escaped near the start of battle, sailed for a short while, then was later captured. One ship of the eight involved in battle, the Nuestra Senora de las Mercedes, also known in translation as Our Lady of Mercy, sunk as a result. She took with her, over a million silver pieces, at least half of copper and a quarter of tin reported in the fleet's cargo manifest.

Two-hundred years pass after Our Lady of Mercy was shown no mercy at the blast of British cannons. Explorers on a mission hunting for the wreck, finally discover it not far from a last known location. Salvage operations commenced, recovering seventeen tons of lost treasure, mostly retrieving bundles of silver coins fused together and a few gold coins with a combined value of roughly five-hundred million; a total of just under six-hundred thousand coins.

According to cargo manifests though, this may be a good portion of what was on board at the time of sinking, but a fair amount of gold and silver plus portions of copper and tin are still unaccounted for. Future dives on the wreck may prove to be prosperous in recovering lost heritage, and perhaps, in discovering the remaining shiny cargo of Mercedes.

Sunken Platinum

Discovery of any lost wreck containing a generous amount of treasure cargo is sure to capture the attention of both seekers and investors alike. Suggesting the find of an erroneous amount though, in the vicinity of three billion, is first met with skepticism and disbelief. In the case of the S.S. Port Nicholson, a great deal of skepticism has resulted from years of salvage attempts with no real evidence to back grandiose claims such as those of treasure hunter Greg Brooks.

Unfortunately for investors in the salvage operations, not only has an implied treasure not been discovered, but evidence to support Greg's claims is thin at best. It is in Brooks' belief the Nicholson was transporting seventy-one tons of platinum, gold ingots, and diamonds as a lender-lease payment to the United States from the Soviet Union.

On contrary to skeptics, there is some merit in Greg's claim, at face value, when looking at the war effort lend-lease arrangements between the United States, Soviet Union, and United Kingdom. The S.S. Port Nicholson was part of the first protocol period whereby supplies were delivered to the Soviet Union by Britain. Some boats utilized in the transport of equipment during the initial lend-lease period war efforts were also used to courier payments on return trip, and remaining payments were granted as interest-free with stipulation to be paid after the war.

This initial period lasted from June to September of 1941, a full year before Nicholson's sinking by a German U-Boat, meaning that in order of the Nicholson to be carrying a lend-lease payment it most likely needed to be an agreed shipment from the original 1941 repayment draft. Lease payments were definitely floating around during this period. Another ship transported payment during the same period, the HMS Edinburgh, and it sunk one month prior to the Nicholson in the Arctic Sea.

However, unlike the HMS Edinburgh transporting four and half tons of gold valued at roughly one-hundred and fifteen million, Brooks claims the Nicholson was carrying significantly more, which many investors now believe to be unlikely for a few reasons. First there is a number of salvage attempts put forth by Brooks without even one recovery or reasonable scrap of proof.

Then we have a salvage crew member stepping forward to describe expedition plans that involve fixing a diver to plant a gold bar for later retrieval with the submersible. It might be understandable given unforeseen difficulties and conditions associated with deep sea salvaging, to require multiple dives before success, but the Brooks operations lasted well beyond investor tolerance. Over time the operation mysteriously changed from a that of a treasure hunt to a routine salvage operation, and this coupled with failure to produce tangible documentation linked to the wreck. These two issues along with the lack in salvage brought about intense scrutiny over the expeditions and backers began to question their investments.

When examining other circumstantial factors it becomes evident the amount of treasure, if any, aboard the Nicholson is far much less than initially claimed. It is documented the ship was transporting fifty-six hundred tons of car parts and military equipment, which means it could quite easily haul seventy odd tons of platinum plus other metals, so there is plausibility in that aspect.

The fact HMS Edinburgh also transported a lend-lease payment during the same period suggests wealth of prominent value found its way to exchange during the war effort. However, it is the type of cargo and amount claimed that becomes concerning when examining global production of platinum at the time.

United States records indicate one and half tons of foreign platinum were imported in 1940, and a further three and half tons in 1941, according to the precious metals production report. If Nicholson made port in New York with the suggested cargo, another seventy tons would've been added as procured by land-lease, jumping by twenty times from the previous year. Not only is this amount a bit high compared to foreign import and domestic production, but also at the time, the Soviet Union entered a commercial agreement with Germany for production materials.

In this agreement Soviet Union agreed to supply various metals, rubber, grains, and two and a half tons of platinum on the material manifest. They shipped the platinum as fifteen-hundred pounds in 1940, then in 1941, another thirteen-hundred pounds; this, for exchange of machinery, armaments, and large tooling.

As the number two producer of platinum in the world, the Soviet Union shipped away at least half of each pound processed in those years, spent in the German deal. With this commercial agreement, Soviet Union would then be paying the United States lend-lease, in one lump sum, with over ten years of store. Considering the production of platinum in the Soviet Union did not escalate until pressure from Germany, it seems unlikely but not entirely impossible.

According to few sources, the Soviet Union may have depleted all of its domestic resources in exchange for machinery from Germany and the United States. Having those resources stretched between two countries, though, makes it that much more difficult for the Soviet Union to fulfilled on their end of the bargain. Even further, for war's duration, the United States supplied eleven billion in deliveries and expected lend-lease payments to account for this.

In 1947, the Soviet Union faced two and half billion after-war repayment, which was then cut in half in 1948, then to eight-hundred million a few years later. Currently, this lend-lease is still outstanding, now reduced to less than seven-hundred million due by the year 2030, proving Russia's reluctance or inability to pay on the debt. This makes it difficult to believe any payments were shipped during the war from Soviet Union to the United States.

Suppose though, if the S.S. Port Nicholson is did transport a payment on its return trip. The United States supplied one-hundred million worth of aid in 1941, and seventy tons of platinum was worth three-hundred and eight million at the time; Now worth three point one billion on today's market. Is it likely the Soviet Union sent a payment for almost four times the amount of supplies received?

Unforgiving Seas

Even in modern times with sophisticated technology, advanced training, and a better scientific understanding of the oceans, treasure may still be lost at sea. Dangerous weather, unfortunate luck, miscalculations or negligence sometimes play key roles in surviving. Risks of transporting cargo over rough seas still remain as they were hundreds and thousands of years ago.

Technology enables modern captains to assess weather conditions from a distance to help minimize that risk, but without following those technological innovations designed to make sailing safer, the risk may introduce even greater dangers. In 2012, a Russian ship by the name of Amurskaya unfortunately met its end due to a combination of these unfortunate circumstances, failing to abide by the limitations of technology and underestimation of the weather, resulting in disaster.

Amurskaya, transporting around seven-hundred and fifty tons of gold ore, worth nearly a quarter million, on its way to make port in Okhotsk. The weight likely played a role in the ship's downfall, twenty-two percent over capacity, one-hundred and forty tons greater than safe limits, sailing into stormy weather stirring over the Sea of Okhotsk.

Port authority gave the Amurskaya a green light, but little did they know what would soon unfold. Reports indicate radio contact was lost near or around the time of sinking, and without communication record, the cause of the accident is attributed to a combination of bad weather along with the ship being significantly over-loaded.

In 1975, a shipping disaster in Lake Superior demonstrates similar characteristics with Russia's loss of the Amurskaya. The SS Edmund Fitzgerald, moving four-thousand tons over capacity, found itself faced with a severe winter storm brewing over the lake. Charting beforehand plotted a course intended to be least impact, knowing in advance of this developing system.

Exactly what happened to the Fitzgerald next is a mystery. It's believed a combination of factors lead to its sinking, but a single cause has yet to be identified. Years later, weather modeling showed the Fitzgerald sailed into the worst part of the storm despite hunkering down near Thunderbay in attempt to have it pass over.

Several theories try to make sense of the Fitzgerald's last voyage, from rogue storm waves to a potential of striking a shoal as possibly indicated by damage on the wreck. Other factors include bearing four-thousand tons additional weight, not utilizing available technology at the time such as a fathometer, and failing to outfit the ship with improved watertight bulkheads allowing it to take on water even with a small puncture.

Approximately twenty-four million on today's market worth of iron ore taconite pellets, twenty-nine thousand tons went down in the incident along with the lives of twenty-nine sailors. Official record states the Fitzgerald sank due to weather conditions even though a large number of factors likely contributed.

Both incidents, the Amurskaya and the Fitzgerald, are reminders even in a modern world with advanced technological innovations that ships are still susceptible to unforgiving seas. Naivety, negligence, or a series of unfortunate events have the ability to sink thousands of tons of treasure and other goods to the sea floor in a moment's notice. It is through tragedies such as these that safety regulations become more strict as technology chases the concept of unsinkable, peering across the distant horizon.

Desert Pearls

When one imagines hospitable conditions of a desert, thoughts often focus on what we know generally of deserts. Dry, barren, dusty wastelands with cacti, snakes, and sometimes a hopeful oasis mirage dancing in the heat on the horizon.

Deserts are an extreme environment capable of evaporating water at dangerous rates during the day while producing life-threatening extreme cold temperatures at night. Scouring any desert for any lost treasure may be a death wish, but to find a prized sunken treasure of a Spanish galleon, in a desert?

For the Salton Sea, such a treasure may truly exist and there might possibly be others given the sea's conditions along with how it was once perceived by sailors. An aerial view reveals evidence the sea was once much larger, and history of the area shows a connection to the Gulf of California, also known as the Sea of Cortez, hundreds of years ago.

There are definitely plenty of locations over the vast Sonoran Desert basin where ships could have disappeared. A unique feature once found here is a tidal bore phenomena capable of drawing water into the basin as a flood surge at high tide, and this is where a few legends of lost treasure in the Salton Sea originate.

Significant to the Sea of Cortez and its connection to the Salton Sea, are these tidal bores. Follow a long winding path, with the help of satellite photography, along Rio Colorado from a wide delta at Isle Montague toward a modern Salton Sea for example. River branches are aligned in the general direction with run-off tributaries flowing inward from the basin rim.

Along with this, the Salton basin extends as far east as Yuma, then to the western edge near Anza-Borrego, all the way to a tip which might have been one day just north of Palm Springs, the entire area once known as Lake Cahuilla centuries ago. Modern dams built upstream, and broken levies have changed natural flow of the Colorado River, causing sediment build-up to effectively cease tidal bore flooding, leaving a much smaller salty sea behind.

In the early seventeenth century, Spanish ships visited the California coast in search of oysters for pearls and for other promising discoveries. Accordingly, one of the ships overflowed in pearls and unfortunately sailed into the Salton basin with intent to find passage directly to the Gulf of Mexico or the Atlantic. At the time, such a passageway through the North American continent was thought to exist as evident on sixteenth century maps.

Instead of finding providence, the ship ran aground as water levels dropped with an outgoing tide, forcing the captain to leave it behind. An event described both as the land coming down to barricade the Sea of Cortez like a giant mudslide, and as water drying up below the ship's hull at such an incredibly disastrous rate the ship is left dry, standing upright on its keel.

A second legend is told by Cahuilla Indians who made home around Lake Cahuilla. The account speaks of a large Spanish galleon appearing in the lake and anchoring just offshore from a Cahuilla settlement. Perceiving the Spanish as a threat, the Cahuilla executed a surprise attack as the Spanish made their way to shore.

After a victorious battle and seizing of the ship, the Cahuilla proceeded to salvage the galleon for treasure and goods. They discovered several large iron-bound chests that eventually proved to be impenetrable, even by brute force. Forceful attempts at opening the irons lead to an accidental break in the ship's anchor line, sending it floating out to sea while in the distance they watched the ship capsize and sink from view.

These however, are only a few accounts of potentially many vessels eventually stranded in the Sonoran Desert and some legends even suggest ships have been lost inland as far from the Sea of Cortez as the Mojave. Similar scenarios start with a ship following the gulf to its end, literally, and is then unable to return to sea. The stories paint a vivid picture describing the basin's devious hidden dangers along with further proof tides may change at any time.

For hundreds of years, an incoming tide mixed into the river delta, pushing a wall of water inland as a tidal bore and ship captains may not have realized this was going on. If the entire sea is raising in elevation at the same time, how would a ship floating upon it see the elevation change without land to as reference?

Probability, legend, and motive suggest the distinct possibility of ancient ships existing somewhere beneath the sands of California's deserts although hardened facts have yet to surface. Suggestive evidence is the fuel for some explorers who lead search parties into the dry heat for a once in a lifetime discovery, but they too haven't found the slightest of clues to keep expeditions funded.

Discovering lost wrecks in the Sonoran, or the Mojave, is met with more difficulty than uncovering sunken ships in the sea. It is truly like finding that proverbial needle, in this case, a splinter of wood in a sea of sand. Looking for anomalies with sonar is out and airborne profiling with GPR only provides contours up to thirty feet deep.

Dust storms, debris, and sandy winds in the desert pile together in dunes as deep as two-hundred meters in some places of the Mojave. Even if an odd-shaped formation resembled a galleon in the desert, there's a likely chance for it to be none other than a pile of accumulated particles.

Intriguing
Treasure Mysteries

For thousands of years, insightful knowledge and precious items have traveled far and wide, across the world's oceans and waterways to be exchanged between distant civilizations. To reach the destination, a number of factors contribute to success or failure of missions. Prominent, skillful navigators and captains manage to build reputations that transcend throughout the ages for their efforts; the course of history forever changed.

Many explorers find thrill in understanding how powerful new discoveries are, and they work equally as diligent to protect harbored secrets. Considering value of goods and knowledge, savvy buccaneers often found intelligent ways to catch competition by surprise covertly, or simply throw them off course with distractive measures. What better way to protect interests as a pirate?

Developing and applying intelligent tactics to routine missions hundreds of years ago enabled the uprising of a pirate republic and a force not to be reckoned with around the world. The same tactics forced privateer and Navy fleets to find methods of outsmarting the outlaws, and pirates perpetuated the cycle by outwitting those opposing forces time and time again.

Eventually, interminable conflict inspired an alternative, and most effective way of protecting knowledge from enemies. By hiding information using cryptic missives and treasure maps, pirates drastically improved chances of keeping information from the authorities, privateers, or scalawags playing both sides.

Hiding knowledge also became leverage and a way out for those who found themselves at mercy to the crown. A map indicating where a stockpile of gold and silver resides may buy a pirate out of the brig, or prevent a meeting with the gallows. At the same time, treasure maps enabled mariners to ditch plunder for later return, or to pass off the location to those in allegiance if the need arise.

Old treasure maps may be difficult to decipher and lead to dead ends as they continuously baffle anyone trying to follow them. Perhaps in this respect, some are maps of maps, or lack a type of key-stone to reveal a secret message. If finding a lost treasure is increasingly difficult with a map in hand, providing at least some sort of direction, just imagine the complexity of discovering buried plunder only known to exist by legend.

Ghost Shipwrecks

To some degree, the idea of a ghost ship is imagined in a literal sense. Much like a mysterious, spectral vessel slowly peering from misty fog as it glides closer, and closer into viewing distance. Once the deck becomes decipherable, you notice nobody aboard, captaining itself above the dark abyss. To this, one may even imagine a translucent crew, skeleton swabbies with curved blades and pirate hats.

This aside, we now ask, what exactly is a ghost ship? To deep sea treasure hunters and wreck divers, ghost ships present unfortunate dead ends and money pits. A figment of legend without historical account and a long cryptic trail to follow. It seems as though ghost ships have existed simultaneously with the real deal since the dawn of salvage operations, possibly even before.

One theory, which is accepted among some researchers, is that of deception in a variety of forms. In modern times, certain vessels classed as ghost ships may be the result of promoters attempting to gain attraction from tourism in areas of mention. Likewise, during pirate days, mentioning the location of a promising wreck while having a few at the pub is possibly one way to misdirect competition into looking elsewhere, far away from your own intended search area. Add salting to the plan and the distraction may work for a longer period of time while building some credibility among pirates and pillagers.

Similar to intentionally marking lagan falsely for later reclamation, the concept of salting is borrowed from dubious gem mining operations; whereby prospectors were sometimes deceived of prosperity by crafty fellow who plant gemstones on a plot in order to sell the supposed claim or rights. It's not too unreasonable to expect the same sort of practice to take place among sea treasure hunters. Throwing a modestly filled chest overboard, may be enough to keep a salvage operation focused on that area for some time.

Aside from the possibility of ghost wrecks as the result of devious treasure hunter shenanigans, there are some points which suggest a level of legitimacy may exist under certain accounts. One of these concepts considers a possible existence of ships repaired or built from miscellaneous wreckage parts at which point the resulting vessel becomes nearly unrecognizable.

At the time pirates ran rampant in the Caribbean, everything and anything useful that could be salvaged from sunken boats found new uses. For the matter of survival, this included at minimum to be the ship's cache, supplies, swords, manifests, rope, sails, and possibly unspoiled food. It is common to find pirate wrecks which show significant signs of modifications, bolstered with added cannons, and outfitted for tactical missions. An unrecognizable vessel may then become a figment of historical record with ties to legend and myth of a lost crew.

Another concept examines the idea of ghost ships from a different perspective altogether. Given the value of wealth transported between the continents, extreme measures were necessary to ensure successful delivery of goods. To keep those transports below medieval pirate radar, there exists a possibility of completely private, undocumented fleets kept secretive by design under order of the crown. In times during civil conflict and attacks on royal thrones, deceptive tactics may have been employed to protect assets coming into the country.

Along with this, there is a distinct possibility ship records may have been lost, stolen, or burned during disputes and the transitioning of power over kingdom rule. We understand a great deal of knowledge was lost in this manor throughout the ages, and with a significant amount of wealth at stake, this concept does remain plausible; with those undocumented and secret transport ships eventually becoming part of a lost history.

Ghost ships are also sometimes referred to as vessels that leave port never to be seen again, leaving little trace in their wake with hardly any evidence to discover where they might have disappeared to. Theories attempting to explain vanished ships involve those commonly attributed to wreck disasters such as bad weather, captain error, a marine heist, or damage to the boat that causes it to take on water.

Sometimes the disappearance is so bizarre that rumors spread with the notion of other-worldly phenomena to blame. Without clues to follow it becomes anyone's guess as to what exactly happened during those last few moments, leaving nothing more than a perplexing mystery for future underwater explorers to attempt explaining.

Lue Map Controversy

Traditionally, pirate loot maps pointing to buried treasure feature an iconic letter X marking the spot, indicating to those reading the map, dig at the point where two lines meet. From the icon, a dashed line leads a path around obstacles directly to the burial site.

Simple maps drawn in this fashion worked for many years, but then as treasure stashing became a well known practice, maps took on more cryptic approaches to help keep it hidden until such time the looter could return. Over time, maps to burial sites were decorated with symbols and jumbled words to help hide the true location, requiring intimate knowledge of the treasure to find it. This practice also inspired lore of the maps themselves, with stories and legends told time and time again describing the location to buried treasure by aid of a map. In some situations, the maps themselves became almost as valued as the loot itself, as though the directions could guarantee treasure.

Yet, maps using cryptic symbols and word phrases to hide a true meaning, eventually proved to be less desirable in a sense by only inspiring an obsession to solve the riddle. Of course there is incentive to solve the problem, but it is the degree of complexity that eventually becomes the most deterring factor. For example, the strange non-traditional Lue Treasure map, which appears to be a collection of Masonic symbols arranged in a way that possibly indicates some sort of direction.

The Lue map is a more modern rendition of an ancient treasure map, and to some researchers, it appears to be incomplete. Beyond this, it is an intriguing story behind it which makes this a little more difficult to decipher, to find fourteen tons of gold were buried somewhere in the United States. To entertain this idea, is supporting evidence available?

Between the first and second world wars, United States economy faced its toughest moments in history. In 1929, the stock market collapsed, adding to an already troubled state steadily escalating from this point. The Great Depression ensued, and many countries around the world faced significant financial hardship over the next two decades. Foreign war campaigns attempted to devalue the US economy while it spiraled during the depression.

To help combat this, Franklin Roosevelt signed a document, entitled the Gold Reserve Act in 1934, to prohibit private possession of gold. Some researchers believe this is where the Lue treasure map stems from, that the Gold Reserve Act is a direct response to German war efforts attempting to inflate, devalue, and destabilize the US economy by introducing large amounts of gold into the financial system.

German war efforts increased substantially in power to the point of war in 1939, and this only furthered attempts to artificially inflate world economies. In 1942, the Germans established an initiative known as Operation Bernhard running out of multiple concentration camps. The goal of this operation, to print enough counterfeit British bank notes to destabilize its economy.

By 1945, Operation Bernhard had produced over one-hundred and thirty-million pounds, but the British learned of the forged currency early enough to take preventative measures comparing bank notes to those recorded in a master ledger. The operation certainly provides insight and credibility to the extent Germany was willing to go in order to destabilize world economies, bolstering conspiracy theories around the Lue treasure map.

Introducing gold to the U.S. economy, however, is presented with a different level of challenge altogether than passing forged notes. German efforts included the procurement of treasures and gold from as many sources possible, but a debatable question comes with those motives. While collecting a large amount of wealth in precious metals, would the Germans really elect to seed a foreign economy with it? Perhaps yes, thinking it may be returned into possession if the effort was successful, or in that wealth truly held little weight in the regime's moral.

Yet the initiative also detracts from Germany's self-empowering righteousness at the time aimed at eradicating anyone who didn't meet their standardized guidelines. There is, of course, logistics of the matter also. How would they physically introduce fourteen tons of gold into the American economy at the time of war, unseen and America unawares?

Sophisticated spy rings might be an answer to this curious question. The Duquesne spy ring and

Operation Pastorius, for example, setup men on U.S. soil for espionage and eventual sabotage. Participants in the spy rings communicated hidden messages in attempt to get crucial inside information back to Germany. Operation Pastorius provides some insight to how twenty-eight thousand pounds of gold possibly landed on American shores, that is, by U-boats.

Knowing that German submarines were dropping off spies, it's not unreasonable to consider gold may be delivered in a similar manor. After that, then it became a matter of injecting the economy with it by spending. According to the story of the Lue treasure map, the gold was transported to a single location for later disbursement, but with the collapse of Germany and the end of the second world war, the gold was left behind.

Then, years later, a cryptic map surfaces which is claimed to detail where a secret stash of gold is located on American soil. What must be considered next is the possibility the Lue Treasure map points to a now empty location. In the height of war, knowing that Roosevelt signed the Gold Act years prior, it would be in the best interest of the U.S. government to obtain the treasure before any attempt to harm the economy took place. Given intelligence efforts in America must have been aware of a plot at this level.

Double agents working within the spy rings for

the US likely obtained information about such an operation if it indeed existed. Thus meaning, chances of finding fourteen tons of gold buried by Germans on American soil in the 1930's are very slim to none if at all. The appearance of the Lue map is so complex, however, that theorists believe government agencies have not deciphered its contents. Which then lends to the idea, of a substantial war treasure existing somewhere in the United States.

There is another possible explanation for the Lue treasure map, one which is opposite from the Germans depositing gold in the U.S. as a means to deflate the economy. The 1934 Gold Reserve Act established that all private gold must be sold to the Treasury. All gold collected during this process was moved to secured facilities around the country. This includes Fort Knox in 1937, after the gold vault was opened. German spies in the U.S. undoubtedly learned of this and perhaps considered these depositories as targets to collapse the economy.

After all, instead of introducing gold to hyper-inflate, removing it is much more effective. This brings about an idea that spies learned of bullion depository locations and used ciphers, like the Lue treasure map, to relay the location back to Germany. During the second world war, gold bullion in the depository is reached an astounding twenty-thousand tons before redistribution among other depositories after the war. The realistic impact of fourteen tons of gold added to twenty-thousand is negligible, but incentive to focus on depositories, much more tantalizing.

Apostle Island Treasure

Early fur trading in the seventeenth century was a booming industry in North America with many types of pelts reaching peak value through demand. By the 1800's this once lucrative industry began to dwindle with animal populations becoming scarce, forcing fur traders into exploring alternate sources of wealth.

As fur trading exploded in popularity, trading posts were established across the continent, connecting resources and wealth into a large network.

Fur outposts became early stores, reliable for a number of other essentials, changing along with the times. A well known Chequamegon trader, by the name of Benjamin Armstrong had done just this.

Armstrong opened a store in La Pointe Wisconsin on Madeline Island, then later established a trading post on Oak Island, north of there. Benjamin traded wood to steamships passing through Lake Superior's Apostle Islands, and various goods such as corn and rye with the Chippewa. Around this time, La Pointe was the commercial hub for western Lake Superior.

Benjamin's trading prowess introduced his family to a number of people around the Apostle Islands including a mysterious hermit. The fellow lived alone on an island between Madeline and Oak, seldom visiting other islands or the mainland. Rumors about the man, last name Wilson, claimed he was well off with more money in coins than he knew what to do with.

The hermit was first encountered at the boat dock on Oak Island, as Wilson sought to obtain a barrel of whiskey. Benjamin obliged, and even went so far as to help him boat the barrel back and receive payment for doing so. Once there, it became evident Wilson really did have a little wealth, pulling out bags of coins for Armstrong to count. This deal lead to future agreements and

Benjamin became a more frequent visitor to trade for hay.

During one of Armstrong's routine boat trips in 1861, he noticed a regular burning fire kept by Wilson, was snuffed out. According to his account, chimney smoke ceased, and after two days with no sign of life from the island he traveled with Judge Bell to find out if Wilson was alright. The two found his body in a scene which appeared to be result of foul play and very little trace of any wealth.

Exactly how many gold and silver coins Wilson owned is unknown, as with its whereabouts to this day. A very small stash of coins were found in the cabin after exhaustive searching, but nothing near the amount as his trading seemed to indicate. People have searched around Hermit Island, and other Apostle Islands with hope of discovering the missing fortune. Where did the coins come from, and where did they go?

One theory about where Wilson may have obtained his coins stems from history of Hermit Island, well before Wilson set foot on the land and called it home. Almost two-hundred years earlier, at the height of the North American fur trade, the Apostle Islands were bustling with activity. A group of pirates in the area sought to capitalize on industry success by targeting passing vessels and trading operations. The pirates made camp using a cave located somewhere on Hermit Island, and presumably stored plunder obtained from endeavors.

Actual identity of the pirates is unknown, and their demise is mentioned as the result of a poorly planned attack on a French fur trading ship. If the pirates indeed cached treasures on the island, this provides a plausible explanation of where Wilson might have obtained a large amount of wealth beyond trading; by finding a lost pirate treasure stashed on the island.

Modern explorers have tirelessly combed the cabin area and surrounding islands without finding a trace of gold. With a near solitary life, it's difficult to determine where Wilson kept his treasure, and there are a number of nooks and shoreline caves throughout the area.

Epilogue

While researching Treasures of the Tropical Variety, a new understanding of heritage once locked fathoms below the sea found its way to the surface. Intriguing and absolutely fascinating mysteries eccentric to a way of life which persists to this day; treasure mysteries that now bring realizations and new understandings.

The world's maritime history is an important part of who we are and a vital way to understand how life was, long before highway corridors, metropolis cities, and before benefits of modern technology. Treasure hunting today is not the same as it was hundreds of years ago even though eighty percent of the world's trade still travels by water. The days of privateers and pirates have steadily succumbed to more civilized practices conscientious of preserving fragile heritage sunken below the seas. Where outlaw and pillagers were once comfortably untouched while profiting off lost treasures, governments have stepped in to protect cultural heritage for the enjoyment of generations to come.

Lives, ships, or treasure lost at sea weigh heavily on society and its economies. The oceans provide passage for people to easily move themselves and goods between continents, but the waters can be dreadfully unforgiving and quick to swallow those who coast across. Legends describing the Kraken may hold merit, not in the sense of an actual ship-devouring sea monster, but as a metaphor of what the vast oceans are ultimately capable of.

It is this, the perseverance of ship captains and their crews determined to make port. Those who fight long hours in unfavorable weather to bring people and supplies across the seas, fulfilling an almost saint-like duty. A diligent plight without doubt a most courageous testament to mankind's ability to adapt and overcome. The ability to navigate and survive some of the greatest expanses of our planet eventually develops into its own way of life, one which brings new worlds, discoveries, and knowledge within reach. Moreover, ship captains and crews over hundreds of years have created opportunity while helping facilitate the advancement of mankind.

Sea faring vessels helped distribute cultures into all four corners of the globe and brought with them supplies to sustain life for some time. Over many years the sailing process has enabled people and technology to flourish. In the face-paced modern world, sea shipping may be easily taken for granted by those not working in directly related professions. The benefits, however, are incredibly significant in that everyone is affected by ocean trade is daily life.

For the casual treasure hunter who humbly respects historical significance, preservation limits an ability to freely explore lost wrecks in hopes of an ultimate payday. Yet, divers still work creatively to find new ways of discovery within those limitations beyond their control. Competition against big exploration corporations with unlimited resources severely hamper the chances of independent divers uncovering the next biggest find of the century. To many underwater explorers, and even select corporations, the thrill isn't necessarily money-orientated, and is instead for discovery itself.

Of course, business ventures are interested first in returns to fund and continue operations, but the admiral driving factor goes beyond the value of any monetary investment. For a treasure hunter to say they found lost heritage, by thoroughly researching and working diligently to realize the goal above all odds, there is a true sense of achievement. To establish and pursue the quest of restoring artifacts of historical importance to civilizations, risking their own life for others to benefit.

Then it is realized, treasure hunting is about its whole contribution to mankind above and beyond monetary worth. For the bigger picture, a purpose of advancing our understanding of past life on the planet and improving underwater archaeology as a respected and necessary science.

To one day turn around, fulfilled in knowing

the efforts helped restore a lost part of history for civilizations who may have not been capable of redeeming it themselves. Then, to make the treasure accessible to the public for enjoyment and education. These are major motivating factors in common, and this point is dearly sincere among respected underwater explorers around the world.

Arthur Kingtide